Strategic
Business
Partner

Other books by the authors:

Performance Consulting

Moving from Training to Performance (coeditors)

Training for Impact

Zap The Gaps! (with Ken Blanchard)

Strategic Business Partner

ALIGNING PEOPLE STRATEGIES WITH BUSINESS GOALS

by

Dana Gaines Robinson
James C. Robinson

BERRETT-KOEHLER PUBLISHERS, INC.
San Francisco

Berret-Koehler Publishers, Inc.

235 Montgomery Street, Suite 650

San Francisco, CA 94104-2916

Tel: (415) 288-0260   Fax: (415) 362-2512   www.bkconnection.com

ORDERING INFORMATION

Quantity sales. Special discounts are available on quantity purchases by corporations, associations, and others. For details, contact the "Special sales Department" at the Berrett-Koehler address above.

Individual sales. Barrett-Koehler publications are available through most bookstores. They can also be ordered directly from Berrett-Koehler: Tel: (800) 929-2929; Fax: (802) 864-7626; www.bkconnection.com

Orders for college textbook/course adoption use. Please contact Berrett-Koehler: Tel: (800) 929-2929; Fax: (802) 864-7626

Orders by U.S. trade bookstores and wholesalers. Please contact Publishers Group West, 1700 fourth Street, Berkeley, CA 94710. Tel: (510) 528-1444; Fax: (510) 528-3444.

Berrett-Koehler and the BK logo are registered trademarks of Berrett-Koehler Publishers, Inc

Printed in the United States of America

Berrett-Koehler books are printed on long-lasting acid-free paper. when it is available, we choose paper that has been manufactured by environmentally responsible processes. These mat include using trees grown in sustainable forests, incorporating recycled paper, minimizing chlorine in bleaching, or recycling the energy produced at the paper mill.

Library of Congress Cataloging-in-Publication Data

Robinson, Dana Gaines, 1944–

   Strategic business partner : aligning people strategies with business goals / by Dana Gaines Robinson and James C. Robinson.

     p. cm.

   Includes bibliographical references and index.

   ISBN 978-1-57675-283-8

   1. Personnel management. 2. Strategic alliances (Business). 3. Strategic planning. I. Robinson, James C., 1930- II. Title.

HF5549.R593 2004

658.3'02--dc22   2004059461

First Edition

10 09 08 07 06 05   10 9 8 7 6 5 4 3 2 1

Production Manager: Susie Yates, Publication Services, Inc.

Supervising Editor: Alysia Cooley, Publication Services, Inc.

Production Coordinator: Sarah Lee, Publication Services, Inc.

Design: Foti Kutil, Publication Services, Inc.

Layout: Steven M. Sansone, Publication Services, Inc.

Contents

Preface

"Human Resources must become more integrated to the business and add value to our organization. It is vital that each of you work more as Strategic Business Partners.
I need you to be 'at the table' with your customers."

For the past decade, statements like this have been made throughout Human Resource (HR) departments in numerous organizations. Multiple journal articles, books, presentations, and research studies have been published affirming the belief that the HR function is key to business success. Consider a recent study completed by Accenture in which business executives ranked the HR function as third, after sales and customer service, as a function that makes a "very significant" contribution to a company's bottom line (2002/2003, p. 12).

There is strong awareness that the HR function must become more strategic and business-linked. Depending upon the study you select, between 50 and 90 percent of HR functions *are* making a transition in this direction. What are the results to date? Unfortunately, results are on the whole disappointing. In the same Accenture study, just 13 percent of the senior corporate executives indicated they were "very satisfied" with overall performance of their HR organization (2002/2003, p. 16). One reason is that many HR functions still operate in a primarily administrative and tactical manner. Edward Lawler III and Susan Mohrman with the Center for Effective Organizations at the University of Southern California in Los Angeles state, "Given the amount of attention to the importance of HR becoming a strategic partner, it is surprising that recent studies have found relatively little change in its activities and structure" (2003, p. 5).

There are many reasons HR functions demonstrate only modest movement toward a more strategic role. One of these reasons is that *strategic HR* and *business partner* are not clearly defined roles. These are esoteric terms that, at a conceptual level, are highly appealing. We describe Strategic Business Partners (SBPs) as people who work with management to define, align, and implement people initiatives to benefit the business. When the partnership is optimized, SBPs contribute to formation of business strategies and plans at the enterprise level. But what is it that SBPs actually do day to day? How is this different from what people do when working in other HR, Learning, and Organization Development (OD) roles? What actions are *proven* to result in earning the right to work with leaders of an organization on business issues and future direction? What *are* the value-added services HR business partners provide once they are working side by side with an organization's leaders? These questions are answered in this book.

Scope of Book

In 1995 we published our book, *Performance Consulting.* Since then we have worked with thousands of HR, Learning, and OD practitioners to fill the role of performance consultant. One of the most frequent questions asked of us is, "How do you get managers to *want* to work with you in this more strategic manner?" The results of our quest to answer that question are contained in this book.

We are behavioral in our approach. In our book, *Performance Consulting*, we provide the reader with the how-to's of making that role real. In this book we use a similar how-to approach focusing on the SBP role within an HR department. We view the terms of being strategic and adding value as conceptual; they are where the rubber meets the sky. In this book we articulate instead where the rubber meets the road. We will discuss the behaviors and actions needed to perform this role in five areas:

- Clarify the difference between a tactical HR function and one that is truly operating in a strategic manner.

- Provide a model of SBPs' accountabilities.

- Discuss proven behavioral practices for building strategic partnerships with clients as well as for partnering with these clients on strategic projects.

- Clarify the added value an SBP brings when "at the table" with an organization's leaders.

- Provide actions that can and must be taken by HR functions if they are to successfully embrace and support a more strategic role within their organizations.

An important distinction to note about this book is that it focuses on the *role* of the SBP. There are numerous books that have described requirements for an HR function to operate strategically—an important subject indeed. Although the last chapter of this book *does* focus on the function and its design to ensure support of the SBP role, the remaining chapters are targeted to you as an individual and what you need to do as an SBP. We aim to answer the question, "What must you do day to day to work successfully as an SBP?"

For Whom Is This Book Written?

You'll note our reference to Human Resources and the term HR. We are viewing this area in its broadest sense, inclusive of the HR, Learning, and OD disciplines practiced today. Essentially, this book is written for people who work in the people side of any organization—for profit, not-for-profit, and public. This book is written from the perspective of someone who works within an organization, whether that organization is small or large. However, most of the techniques and practices are relevant to those individuals who work externally in a consultative role. This book is for you if your job title or role is comparable to any of the following:

Individual Contributor Roles	*Leader Roles*
Benefits Advisor	Chief Learning Officer
Compensation Analyst	Director or VP, Human Resources
HR Advisor	Manager, Human Resources
HR Business Partner	Manager, Center of Excellence
HR Generalist	Manager, Organization Development
HR Specialist	or Organization Effectiveness
Learning Strategist	Manager, Training and Development
OD Consultant	
Performance Consultant	
Recruitment Specialist	
Trainer	

This book will also be helpful to people considering a career change into HR with an eye to a more strategic role. This book provides insight into what SBPs do day to day, identifies the benefits and challenges encountered, and articulates the competencies needed to perform the SBP role successfully.

Overview of the Contents

This book is divided into four sections. In Part One we discuss the four key concepts underpinning a strategic HR approach. Additionally, the accountabilities for SBPs are introduced.

The focus of Part Two is on actions successful SBPs take as they build partnerships with line manager clients, a fundamental SBP accountability. You'll learn specific practices that successful business partners use to ACT: gain Access, grow Credibility, and develop Trust. These three elements are required to build strategic relationships and to be viewed as someone who can add value to the business. These relationships are what open the door to strategic opportunities.

Part Three describes techniques SBPs use to identify and support specific opportunities and projects. Working on strategic projects is another SBP accountability. The logic used to ask "the right questions right" is discussed as are tactics to identify strategic projects both reactively and proactively.

Part Four focuses on the third accountability of what SBPs, who are at the executive table, do to add value. Of specific importance is how SBPs contribute to development of strategic business plans, integrating the HR strategic plan and people initiatives into those plans. We conclude the book with actions required of HR leaders to design a department supportive of strategic work, enabling some HR team members to operate as SBPs.

SBP Tools and Examples

Our intent is to make this book practical and filled with many how-to's. We include checklists and behavioral suggestions, such as lists of questions to use when partnering with your clients. In this way the book is both informative and educational.

Here are some of the other elements of the book you may find of interest:

- *Something You Can Do* are exercises you may elect to complete as a way of applying the concepts that you read about in the chapter.
- *SBP Examples* appear throughout the book and tell stories of actual applications of techniques discussed in this book.

There are many lessons to be learned from both the successes and problems described.

- *Tools* appear at the conclusion of this book. These are interview guides and models that can be copied and used in your own strategic work.

- *Resources* is a comprehensive list of books to utilize as you continue learning about the strategic business partnering role.

Acknowledgments

Writing a book can be a daunting project. This book would not have been possible without the assistance and support of many people. We certainly want to thank the many clients with whom we have had the privilege to work over the past several years. It is through the work with these clients, and with their gracious support, that we have been able to form and test the many practices and techniques included in this book.

We also want to thank the members of our talented team at Partners in Change, Inc.: Terri Lutz, Heather Rudar, and Linda Venturella. As a result of their skill and competence, we have been provided with periods of time when we could remove ourselves from the day-to-day pressures of a business and concentrate on writing this book. Special thanks to Heather Rudar for the many hours she has spent inputting our drafts (which sometimes looked like a roadmap!) into documents that are legible, enhanced, and articulate. And we want to acknowledge Terri Lutz for her creative talents in designing the graphic that appears in this book as well as her review of the final manuscript to ensure that consistency reigned. As someone who works with our firm on occasion, we also want to thank Linda Robinson for a terrific job of identifying books to include in the Resources section.

Throughout the book you'll find many examples from people who are working in the role of SBP in their respective organizations. We want to thank each of the following individuals who provided these examples for us to share: Kevin Brady, Tom Diamond, Cam Graham, Jill Jennings, Bob Leininger, Cathy Malear, Kevin McNamara, Darryl Middleton, Gayle Miller, Mary Morand, Valerie Norton, Janice Simmons, Barbara Thornton, Bob Waters, Gwynne Whitley, and Mike Woerner.

We also want to thank those individuals who reviewed some or all of the initial draft of our manuscript, providing helpful suggestions for its enhancement. Thanks to Ela Aktay Booty, Marcia Daszko, Kathleen Epperson, Cam Graham, Dave Grof, Susan Hewitt, Kevin McNamara, Gayle Miller, Jill Muehrcke, Jayne Williams, and Vern Williams. And we certainly want to acknowledge the joy of working with Steve Piersanti and his team at Berrett-Koehler. In our opinion there is no finer publisher with whom to work.

Finally, we want to thank each other. We are a professional couple who have worked together for more than 20 years. It is the blend of our individual perspectives that, we believe, adds to the richness of the final product. We know that working together adds immensely to the richness of our working lives.

Pittsburgh, PA Dana Robinson
December 2004 Jim Robinson

Introduction

From Value Sapping to Value Adding

In 1996 a column appeared in *Fortune* magazine that created quite a stir within the Human Resource (HR) profession. Entitled "Taking on the Last Bureaucracy," the column's author indicated that he had a modest proposal regarding the HR department. "Why not blow the sucker up? I don't mean improve HR . . . I mean abolish it" (Stewart, 1996, p. 105).

These are tough words! Could they be an anomaly, stated by someone who had a conflict with his local HR department? Unfortunately, it does not appear so. David Ulrich, an esteemed academic, consultant, and supporter of the HR profession, indicated that "as much as I like HR people . . . I must agree that there is good reason for HR's beleaguered reputation. It is often ineffective, incompetent and costly; in a phrase it is value sapping" (1998, p. 124).

Why the criticism of a field that is dedicated to supporting people within organizations? We believe it is largely due to the reticence, even resistance, of many HR functions and professionals to embrace a more strategic, and less transactional,

1

approach. A recent survey of HR professionals by the Society for Human Resource Management (SHRM) indicated that only 7 percent of respondents believed the need for HR to work as a Strategic Business Partner (SBP) was a key trend (Caudron, 2003, p. 28). Higher on the list were managing diversity and administering health care. And while many in the HR field are slow to accept the need to be more strategic, transactional work—the work that has been a primary focus for HR functions—is increasingly being outsourced. According to a research report by SHRM published in 2004, almost 60 percent of organizations responding to the survey indicate that they are currently outsourcing at least one HR function. Many of the most common functions outsourced are transactional and administrative in nature, including employee assistance and counseling, health benefits administration, and temporary staffing (Esen and SHRM, 2004, pp. 1 and 3).

Clearly, expectations for HR are changing. The bar is rising. The result is a gap between what managers and employees need from their HR departments and what is being provided.

A Look Back

It is important to place the current requirements for HR functions within a context. The future of any profession is rooted in its past. Before the 1970s the department was referred to as *Personnel*. Its primary role was to maintain employee records and information. A term frequently used for this function was "corporate attic" because, when there was no obvious place where a task might be assigned, the task was often placed into the Personnel department. That is how many of these departments came to "own" responsibility for the company picnic and the maintenance of organization charts. A highly effective Personnel department in those years was responsive to a myriad of requests, primarily transactional and administrative in nature. The department worked from a "respond to what is urgent" mentality. Knowledge of the "business of the business" was not on the radar screen as a requirement.

Much changed in the next 25 years, as symbolized by the change in the function's name from Personnel to Human Resources. During this time the people issues to manage became much more complex. Legislation to "protect" workers regarding such issues as occupational health, safety, pay, and employment equity proliferated. It was not uncommon to place a lawyer into the lead position within the HR function. Thus was born the HR role of "employee advocate."

Also within this timeframe, HR functions broadened their mission. Organization development, change management, and diversity were added to the traditional HR services of recruitment and benefits administration. Most HR functions were organized into specialties, resulting in a somewhat siloed department. Many HR professionals specialized in one discipline such as learning, compensation or recruitment. Some people became generalists. Still the function worked more from a "respond to the urgent" rather than "focus on the important" approach.

During this time, the needs to be strategic and linked to the business were still not priorities. To some degree this was because many managers and leaders did not expect HR to understand the business. We recall one head of HR who began work in a medical supply company. Within the first month of her employment, she made an appointment to meet with the president of the company. In the discussion, she asked this leader questions about the business goals and challenges for the organization. Just a few minutes into the conversation, the president paused with the question, "Aren't you from HR? Why do you need to ask me questions about the business?"

The "New" HR

Times have changed! Organizations are operating in a much more complex, competitive, and challenging environment.

Many of these challenges directly target the human side of business, with resulting implications for the HR function. Consider the following:

- Organizations must retain and optimize talent. Talent is often viewed as both the number one expense *and* asset of a business. The goal is to have the right person in the right job at the right time, and to do this globally. No small task—but one that HR is expected to lead.

- Successfully managing organizational change is a key requirement for businesses today. Consider all the alliances, joint ventures, acquisitions, and divestitures that occur today and require a change strategy. People in HR are viewed as those who *should* know how to integrate change successfully into the workplace.

- Technology and outsourcing services now available provide options for completing transactional and administrative tasks, such as payroll administration and maintenance of employee records. Although important, these tasks add limited value to the future success of an organization. HR functions are *expected* to utilize alternatives when possible, off-loading the more transactional tasks that characterized HR work in previous decades and on-loading the strategic work now required.

Clearly the requirements placed upon HR functions, and for those who work within them, have changed significantly. In addition to the more traditional requirements, which include recruitment, compensation, and training, HR departments must operate more strategically and proactively. By strategic we mean that the majority of HR time and resources is focused to optimize workplace performance in order to maximize the results of the organization. HR departments must be accountable not for what they *do* but for the results they are providing—from providing *perceived* value to demonstrating *actual* value to the business.

For an HR function to operate strategically, *some* people within the department will need to work in the role of strategic business partner, or SBP, as it is referenced in this book. Specifically, SBPs:

- Partner with middle- and senior-level managers, developing deep knowledge of the business requirements and challenges these individuals face. In essence, SBPs develop access, credibility, and trust with these leaders.

- Identify and partner with their clients to support strategic projects that directly address one or more business need(s) of the organization. This is a project-focused role.

- By performing the first two accountabilities effectively, some SBPs will earn the right to sit "at the table" with their clients. In this accountability the SBP is focusing not on specific projects but on needs of the entire enterprise over a period of years. SBPs who work in this way contribute to formation of business strategies, integrating and executing people initiatives in support of the organization's business plan.

A Compelling Future

Historically, many within the HR profession have lamented the lack of respect and acknowledgment for the services they provide. Now opportunity is banging at the door of every HR function to reverse that situation. The need to be more strategic and business-linked is evident. When an HR function operates in this manner, the results are irrefutable. A 1998 examination of 740 corporations concluded that firms with the greatest intensity of HR practices that reinforce and support performance had the highest market value per employee (Stolz, 2004, p. 21). A study conducted in Australia and again in the United Kingdom by Andersen Human Capital concluded that companies with an HR director on the executive committee evidenced a median annual growth in earnings per share of 13 percent over a five-year period, compared with just 5 percent for companies without HR representation at this level (*Canadian HR Reporter,* downloaded from hrreporter.com on July 24, 2003).

So, the opportunity is here—now. The choice is ours to make—now. The HR profession is at the proverbial fork in the road: to continue to operate transactionally or to step up to the bar and evidence a strategic, business-focused operation. It will mean changes for the entire HR function, requiring that some people, within that group, work as SBPs. Making the choice in favor of strategic HR ensures we are adding value—an aspiration for many. In this regard we certainly support David Ulrich when he said, "Despite the growing pains, the future of HR is phenomenal" (Bates, 2002, p.32).

PART ONE

CONCEPTS AND A MODEL FOR STRATEGIC BUSINESS PARTNERS

Strategic Business Partners (SBPs) demonstrate competence in many ways—through their questioning of clients, their knowledge of the business, and their ability to translate business needs into performance requirements and people initiatives. But performing effectively as an SBP requires use of a mental model as a guide or rudder.

In Chapter 1 we discuss the four key concepts integral to this mental model and critical to success as an SBP. We clarify the nature of strategic work and why an SBP must be involved in strategic initiatives. We also discuss the four types of needs in every organization and why an SBP must be aware of their impact upon every project. In addition we describe how asking the "right" questions and gaining access to clients will have a direct impact upon your success as an SBP.

In Chapter 2 we describe the key accountabilities of SBPs. Acknowledging that these accountabilities are additive, we see them as a high-level model of what successful SBPs do. The first accountability, Build Client Partnerships, is the foundation for the other two. The second accountability, Identify and Partner to Support Strategic Projects, often provides the experience and visibility required for the third accountability, Influence Business Strategies and Direction.

Chapter 1

Key Concepts for Partnering Strategically

> "I just learned that I am going to be working in the role of a Strategic Business Partner. Sounds great, doesn't it? Unfortunately, I'm not certain what it is that I will do differently. Guess it means I will be implementing different solutions than I used to do."

We have had numerous conversations with people in Human Resource (HR) and Training and Development functions that resonate with the preceding statement. To be viewed as a *business partner*, and to do work that is *strategic*, has high appeal. But, as the old adage indicates, "The devil's in the details!"

In this book, we plan to answer the question, "What do you as a Strategic Business Partner (SBP) do differently Monday morning at 8:00 A.M.?" But it is not as simple as providing the top ten proven practices! There will always be situations that have never been encountered before as well as those to be viewed in a different light. You need to draw upon your knowledge of key concepts and accountabilities to determine the practices to use in each unique strategic

9

opportunity. These concepts and accountabilities are the foundation of your role as an SBP.

Overview of Four SBP Concepts

The word *concept* means "a general idea derived or inferred from specific instances or occurrences." From our work and that of academicians and other practitioners in our field, there are clearly four concepts that are relevant to an SBP:

1. *Three Kinds of Work.* HR functions support three kinds of work: transactional, tactical, and strategic. Although SBPs perform all three kinds of work, it is vital that the majority of their work be strategic in nature.

2. *The Need Hierarchy.* If you have read either *Performance Consulting: Moving Beyond Training,* or *Zap the Gaps! Target Higher Performance and Achieve It!,* you will be familiar with this concept, which acknowledges the four needs resident within organizations at all times. This hierarchy will be explained in this chapter; it is a key tool SBPs use to define and align these needs.

3. *Translating Business Needs into Human Performance Requirements and Initiatives.* This concept supports the types of questions that are asked by SBPs. It is vital that SBPs ask "the right questions right" to determine the human performance requirements and gaps relative to a business need. Only then can the most appropriate initiatives be identified. But what are the right questions? They are rooted within this concept.

4. *Identifying the True Client.* One of the most common errors made by SBPs is to learn too late they are not working with the "true" client. Who qualifies as a client? Using appropriate criteria to determine the specific individuals with whom to partner is critical.

Concept One: Three Kinds of Work or "What Is Strategic Work Anyway?"

There are three kinds of work required of those who work in HR, Learning, and Organizational Development (OD) functions: transactional, tactical, and strategic. It seems obvious to say that SBPs should focus on *strategic* work. But it is also safe to say there is lack of shared understanding as to what qualifies as strategic work. Let's begin by discussing the two types of work that are *not* strategic.

Transactional work is sometimes referred to as administrative work. This work is completed in an order-taking manner, with quick turnaround expected. Generally, this work identifies and addresses the needs of individuals. Examples of transactional work typically completed within HR functions include:

- Upgrading an individual employee's HR records.

- Filling a specific position that has been vacated.

- Assisting someone in locating a training program to address a developmental need.

- Counseling a supervisor on how to manage a discussion with an employee whose performance is substandard.

The problem with transactional work is that there is so much of it! To illustrate this point, how many total employees are you currently supporting in your role? Less than 100? More than 1,000? Whichever is the case, consider the number of people who could potentially call each day requesting some type of assistance. You can quickly see why those in HR functions sometimes feel they are buried in transactional work. The dilemma: this category of work will not go away. It must be completed in a competent manner if people in HR are to earn the right to move into the strategic arena. As one operations manager indicated to us, "Why would I invite people in HR to help with my strategic business needs when they can't even get my employees' paychecks done correctly?" Completing transactional work both effectively and in a timely manner is a requirement for earning credibility to work strategically. In Chapter 10 we will discuss some of the structural options used to manage this category of work—options that include Shared Service Centers and outsourcing. For now, we want to clarify what transactional work *looks* like and indicate that it is *not* what SBPs should spend their time doing.

A second category of work completed by HR functions is *tactical*. We actually prefer to think of this type of work as the many *solutions* that are offered. Consider:

- Recruitment initiatives.
- Training programs.
- Restructuring of departments.
- Succession planning processes.

Each of these is a solution—or *tactic*—used to achieve some type of goal. Therefore, *tactical* work results in the design and/or purchase and implementation of HR, OD, and Learning solutions. This work identifies and addresses the needs of work groups. Tactical work has been the home turf for HR functions during the past 20 years. Many HR functions are siloed into solution specialties, such as compensation and benefits, recruitment and staffing, learning and development. If your job title is Compensation Manager or Learning and Development Manager, is it any surprise that clients call you with a solution in mind?

What is interesting about tactical work is the process used to implement it. Tactical work can be implemented in a programmatic manner ("We are rolling out a new leadership training program.") or as part of an overarching strategic initiative ("We are creating greater flexibility in the workforce to support our goals relative to operational efficiency. For this to succeed, our managers need to operate in a more empowering and flexible manner, so we are implementing a leadership development program to build their capability in this area.").

Tactical work can consume a great amount of a person's time. Fortunately, there are many trends in place regarding alternative ways to deliver the tactics and solutions needed while still providing some HR people with the time they require to work as SBPs. These alternatives will be discussed in Chapter 10.

The third and last category of work completed by HR functions is *strategic* work. We define strategic work as work that moves the business into a favorable position, supporting one or more courses of action developed by the organization's leaders. Strategic work identifies and addresses the needs of business entities, including the entire enterprise. Strategic work:

- Focuses on departments, functions, and/or the entire enterprise—it is macro, not micro, in focus.

- Is long-term in scope, often looking out two or more years rather than on the next quarter.

- Is directly linked to one or more business goals of the organization.

- Is solution-neutral in the early stages of partnering.

- Requires multiple solutions or tactics to be implemented; single solutions do not yield results in strategic initiatives.

This is the type of work that, as an SBP, you need to seek to identify and deliver. Examples of working strategically include:

- Partnering with clients to develop business strategies and plans.
- Translating business strategies and goals into human performance requirements.
- Helping to identify *all* the solutions required to enhance performance of people and to positively impact upon the business.
- Supporting the execution of business plans once they are designed.

In summary, keep this in mind:

- Transactional work benefits individuals.
- Tactical work benefits employee work groups.
- Strategic work benefits business units and, perhaps, the entire enterprise.

Something You Can Do

What percentage of your current work is transactional? tactical? strategic? You may want to take a moment to jot down your estimate here, ensuring that the percentages total 100%.

____ % of my work is Transactional.

____ % of my work is Tactical.

____ % of my work is Strategic.

____ % of my work is for other responsibilities.

We do not have an ideal percentage for each category to offer, but we do know that effective SBPs do little (if any) transactional work. The tactical work SBPs do is typically integrated into a strategic initiative rather than positioned as a stand-alone event. It is difficult for you to be viewed as an SBP if clients observe that most of your time is spent recruiting candidates or conducting training programs. You risk being viewed as an expert in that single solution and not a strategic partner to address business needs.

Concept Two: The Need Hierarchy or "What Do SBPs Discuss With Clients?"

Our short-form description of what SBPs do is that they partner with their clients to define and align the four needs of the organization regarding specific business strategies and goals. So, what are these *four* needs?

As Figure 1.1 illustrates, the four needs are business, performance, work environment, and capability. These needs nest like boxes within a box, with the business needs residing at the top of this hierarchy. *Business needs* are the highest-order need because all other needs *should* emanate from them. If business needs go unmet for a protracted period of time, the future of the enterprise is threatened. What are business needs? They have three characteristics:

- Operational in focus.
- Measured in a quantifiable manner.
- Needs or goals for an entity, such as a unit, department, function, plant, or organization.

Figure 1.1 Need Hierarchy

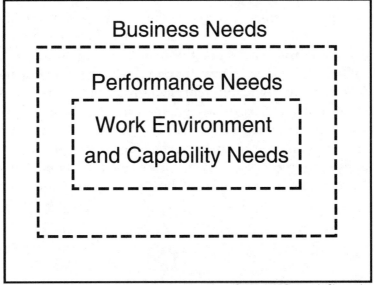

Examples of business needs are to:

- Grow market share.
- Increase profitability.
- Decrease production waste.
- Reduce operational costs.
- Enhance plant safety.
- Improve customer satisfaction.

Each of these is operational, measured numerically, and focused at an entity level, requiring efforts of multiple people in order to be achieved.

Performance needs identify the on-the-job behavior or activities that employees must do (perform) if the business needs are to be successfully achieved. In essence, performance needs answer the questions, "What must people do more, better, or differently if we are to achieve our business goal?" and "How does that compare to what people are typically doing now?" Performance needs require that one or more specific *groups of employees* be identified. By *employee group* we are referencing individuals who share a common job and/or role and who, through their day-to-day performance, most *directly* contribute to the achievement of the business needs. Account representatives, plant managers, and customer service representatives are examples of *jobs* that qualify as employee groups. The key is to identify specific groups and specific behaviors needed by people in these groups—the more specific the practices, the better. Table 1.1 provides some examples of how performance and business needs can be linked.

Table 1.1 Linking Business and Performance Needs

Business Need	Employee Group and Appropriate Performance Needs
Increase revenue	*Sales representatives* need to tier their customers into A, B, and C groupings. They then need to build account penetration plans for customers in the A Group—those customers currently generating at least $1 million or more of revenue per year with our organization.
Increase customer satisfaction	*Customer service representatives* (CSRs) need to ask open-ended questions of customers to identify their specific needs. Then the CSRs should summarize what they have learned to ensure mutual understanding.

Work environment needs represent the infrastructure of the organization surrounding all employees. This infrastructure includes work processes, information flow, reward and recognition systems, as well as clarity of expectations. Many work environment needs are intangible. Although you cannot "see" them, you can always "feel" their presence.

Capability needs are the skills and knowledge employees need to perform effectively. Capability needs also include inherent capability—the background experience, education, traits, and characteristics that are hard-wired into each person. Let's look more closely at work environment and capability needs.

In 2002 we co-authored a book with Ken Blanchard. The book, entitled *Zap the Gaps! Target Higher Performance and Achieve It!*, tells the story of a leader with a business problem in the area of customer service. Working with his HR Manager, this Call Center Director uses The Gap Zapper to identify root causes for the performance problems within a call center. This tool is displayed in Figure 1.2. Essentially, The Gap Zapper is a comprehensive list of most factors that impact upon human performance in the workplace.

External factors are outside the control of anyone in an organization, including the president and board of directors.

Figure 1.2 The Gap Zapper

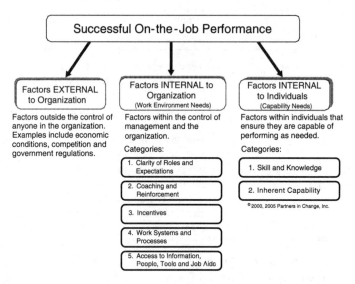

These factors make achievement of performance and business results more difficult, requiring strategies to be formed that will ensure business success despite these factors. Examples of external factors are competitive pressures, economic conditions, and relevant government regulations.

Factors internal to the organization consist of five categories of work environment needs. When these factors are present in a positive manner, they enable performance. When they are either absent or an obstacle, they hinder performance. Note, however, that these factors are something that people in an organization *could* change if they so desired. They are within the control of the organization.

1. *Clarity of Roles and Expectations* focus on employees knowing specifically what their roles and responsibilities are relative to their job goals and accountabilities. This also means that people know how their responsibilities differ from others who are working on the same business goal.

2. *Coaching and Reinforcement* means having a system that provides coaching support to people as they perform their job responsibilities. It also means reinforcing and acknowledging good performance as well as providing developmental feedback when needed.

3. *Incentives* are the rewards, both tangible and intangible, that encourage people to perform as needed. This category requires presence of a positive balance of consequences. When there is lack of any consequence, performance often does not change. It is easy for employees to maintain the status quo when there are no consequences—positive or negative—for changing on-the-job performance.

4. *Work Systems and Processes* are the workflow and organizational systems within which people operate. These can make work performance easier and more efficient, or more difficult and ineffective. Geary Rummler, co-author of the book, *Improving Performance: How to Manage the White Space on the Organization Chart,* stated it quite succinctly when he said, "If you pit a good employee against a bad system, the system will win almost every time" (Rummler and Brache, 1995, p. 75).

5. *Access to Information, People, Tools, and Job Aids* is a category of work environment needs that continues to grow in importance as people are expected to perform in an autonomous manner—without a lot of day-to-day guidance. How can people perform effectively without accurate and current information and access to the type of tools required to do the job?

Factors internal to individuals refer to capability needs. They address factors within individuals that enable people to perform as needed. Once again, these factors are within the control of the organization:

1. *Skill and Knowledge* is the only root cause for which training is an appropriate solution. People cannot perform successfully on the job if they do not know how.

2. *Inherent Capability* relates to the raw ingredient that is within each of us, making each of us unique. This category of capability need is very difficult to develop; it is much more efficient if the selection process accurately identifies people with the required inherent capability.

It is important to note that skill is *not* performance. For example, if a manager called and asked you to develop the negotiating skills of the work team, this manager has provided you with a capability need—not a performance need. To qualify as a performance need, the request must focus on what people are expected to actually *do* on the job as they negotiate.

A question we are frequently asked is, "Where does job motivation fit into this model?" Let us respond to that question here, should you wonder about it also. We view job motivation as a *symptom* and not as a *root cause* of a performance problem. A symptom is an indication that there is a problem. However, a symptom lacks specificity. You must ask questions to determine the root causes of the problem before you can determine a solution that will correct the problem. In this example, you might ask, "Why are people not motivated to perform as needed?" Some of the reasons could be:

• There is little recognition for performing as needed (work environment factor).

• There is a poor job match between what the people can do and what they have been hired to do (capability need).

The same rationale applies to "lack of time" as a reason. What factors are limiting time to focus on a specific performance requirement? Once the root cause(s) of poor job motivation or lack of time have been identified, you can implement appropriate solutions.

The Need Hierarchy visually demonstrates that business and performance needs are the *results* to be achieved. The root causes of nonperformance usually reside in work environment and capability needs. Therefore, most solutions are designed to address the causes found in these two categories. Most HR people have a goal to link their work to the business needs of the organization they are supporting. But, as the Need Hierarchy illustrates, solutions (such as a revised compensation system or a learning program) are not *directly* linked to business needs. Rather, these solutions affect a change in performance that in turn yields results to the business. Therefore, HR groups that want to impact operational results *must* be in the business of changing people's performance.

Something You Can Do

A key skill for you as an SBP is to discriminate between and among the needs within the Need Hierarchy. The first step is to identify which needs have been provided to you by your client. The purpose of this exercise is to provide you with practice in discriminating among the four needs we have been discussing.

Discriminating among Business, Performance, Work Environment, and Capability Needs

Instructions:

- Consider each of the following statements as a request from a client. Each statement is a description of the need as presented by the client. The statements have been sent to you via voice mail, e-mail, or memo. Using only the information in the client's statement, determine what need or needs the client is describing. Make no assumptions.

- Each of the statements identifies one or a combination of the following needs:

BN = Business Need. The statement defines operational goals or needs of the organization. The statement may or may not contain the numerical measures; however, that information could be obtained by questioning the client.

PN = Performance Need. The statement defines what people must do on the job and/or what they are currently doing. The descriptors may be vague, but on-the-job behavior is clearly the focus.

WN/S = Work Environment Need or Solution. The statement identifies one or more of the five categories of work environment needs described in The Gap Zapper and/or it provides a solution that addresses one of these needs.

CN/S = Capability Need or Solution. This is a statement that identifies the skill, knowledge, and/or inherent capability required of people or it describes what is lacking in this regard. The statement may also provide a solution to address this category of cause.

- After you have made your selections, turn to the end of this chapter to see how your answers compare to ours.

1. We are in the process of reducing operational expenses in our service centers. Can you help us put together a communication program to help people in the centers understand why we are doing this?

   ___ BN   ___ PN   ___ WN/S   ___ CN/S

2. The managers in my region are skillful in the technical area. What I need to do is improve their interpersonal skills. They are not communicating with nor managing their teams in a satisfactory manner.

   ___ BN   ___ PN   ___ WN/S   ___ CN/S

3. We plan to increase revenue in the next year. We must ensure our talent recruitment and retention processes are ready as we need everyone performing in an optimal manner to reach our goal.

___ BN ___ PN ___ WN/S ___ CN/S

4. Our sales representatives are not focusing on the long-term strategic sales that we need in this business. I'd like to talk to you about a new sales incentive program that would offer greater rewards for this kind of sale.

___ BN ___ PN ___ WN/S ___ CN/S

Concept Three: Translating Business Needs into Human Performance Requirements or "What Questions Do I Ask?"

Asking "the right questions right" is a critical skill for SBPs. The questioning process, more than any other single process, helps to translate business needs into performance requirements. Essentially, you can raise concerns and influence clients more by what you ask than by what you tell. The questioning techniques will be discussed more thoroughly in Chapters 6 and 7; for now we want to introduce the three types of questions to be asked: SHOULD, IS, and CAUSE.

- *SHOULD questions* identify both the business and performance "SHOULDs" or desired state. Business SHOULDs are described numerically ("increase revenue by 10 percent") and performance SHOULDs are defined behaviorally ("use the tables feature in Microsoft® Word").

- *IS questions* identify what currently exists compared to the SHOULDs. Business IS information describes current results in quantifiable terms ("our revenue is currently increasing at a rate of 6 percent"), whereas IS performance defines the current behavior of specific employee groups ("engineers are not using the tables feature in Word").

- *CAUSE questions* focus on the root causes for why people are not performing as required. They also identify factors that might hinder future performance once a new initiative is underway. CAUSE questions draw upon the content in The Gap Zapper.

We have developed an acronym to assist in recalling the types of questions to be asked. The acronym is GAPS! and works in this manner:

G = **G**o for the SHOULD

A = **A**nalyze the IS

P = **P**in down the CAUSES

S = **S**elect the right SOLUTIONS

When the GAPS! acronym is integrated into the Need Hierarchy, as Figure 1.3 illustrates, the type of questions to ask become evident.

SHOULD and IS questions help to translate business needs into performance needs. CAUSE questions go below symptoms to identify root causes for problems. Root causes lead to identification of the solutions required to address the problem. In this way alignment among the four needs is accomplished.

SBP Example

Asking the Right Questions

Marilyn, an SBP within a large pharmaceutical company, was assigned to support clients within a major business unit within the organization. Marilyn thoughtfully identified those individuals with whom she needed to build strategic client partnerships. She scheduled an initial meeting with each client and continued to grow the relationships over time. Several months after she began growing these

Figure 1.3 GAPS! Process and the Need Hierarchy

G = *Go* for the SHOULD

    Ask SHOULD questions to determine:
- ✓ Business goals
- ✓ Performance requirements

> Business SHOULD Questions
> Performance SHOULD Questions

A = *Analyze* the IS

    Ask IS questions to clarify:
- ✓ Current business results
- ✓ Actual performance

> Business IS Questions
> Performance IS Questions

P = *Pin down* the CAUSES

    Ask CAUSE questions to discover:
- ✓ Work environment support
- ✓ Capability of individuals

> Work Environment and Capability Causes Questions

S = *Select* the right SOLUTIONS

    Select and implement two categories of solutions:
- ✓ Work environment support
- ✓ Capability solutions

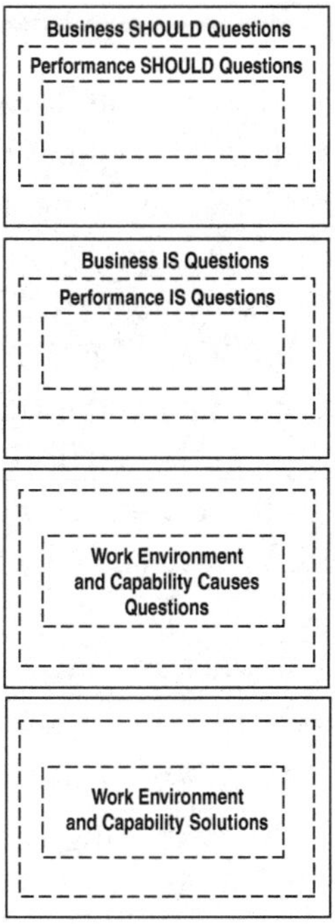

> Work Environment and Capability Solutions

relationships, the president of the business unit called and asked her to obtain the dates for all future operating committee meetings. These are meetings the president held monthly with his senior team. The president wanted Marilyn to begin attending these meetings. She was, in essence, being invited "to the table." Marilyn responded, "I will be pleased to attend. I will contact Louise today to obtain the dates and get them on my calendar. But I'm curious, why do you want me to attend these meetings?" His response: "I want you there because of the *questions* you ask us. You have caused us to think about how to align performance of our people with requirements of the business in ways we have not thought about before—and need to do more of in the future." Essentially, she was invited to the table because of the questions she asked!

Concept Four: Determining the Client or "Who to Partner With?"

Let us share one of our frequent experiences. When we ask our clients in HR whom they view as *their* clients, we receive a myriad of responses including "all employees," "all managers," and even "our organization's customers." Clearly the word *client* is not universally defined nor understood! Suffice it to say that there is no way that you can strategically partner with *all* of any one group—unless the organization is relatively small. Considering the potential payback, it is vital that you invest time partnering with those within your organization who can make things happen. We define "clients" as individuals who:

- Own (have accountability for) achieving business results within the organization.

- Have authority or power to make things happen, including the garnering of resources required to support a specific initiative.

- Are within the chain of command of the employees whose performance is to be changed in some manner.

Interestingly, clients come in two flavors: sustained and project. *Sustained clients* meet the criteria in the preceding list because of their position and influence power within the organization. You develop and maintain a partnership with them independent of any current project or initiative. Generally, sustained clients are located in the mid to upper levels of the organization. Job titles of sustained clients often include President, Chief Executive Officer, Vice President, Chief Operating Officer, General Manager, Country Manager, and Director. As one SBP indicated, "I view the President and his direct reports as my sustained clients."

Project clients, by contrast, meet the criteria noted for a specific project. These are individuals whose position and power generally do not warrant a sustained partnership. However, the importance of their role relative to a specific project does warrant a relationship. Often project clients are really *client teams* where several individuals have some ownership for the business and performance results associated with the project. For example, if the business need is to introduce a new product to the marketplace, a client team may consist of the Vice President of Sales, Vice President of Marketing, and Vice President of Supply Chain Management. Client teams are almost always required for enterprise-wide projects. Although a sustained client may work as a project client, the reverse is not necessarily true. Your level of contact with project clients is strong during the life of the project but will decline once the project has concluded.

The implication is that it would be valuable for you to identify those individuals with whom you wish to build a sustained partnership. Then work to gain access to and develop credibility and trust with these individuals. We will discuss how to do this in Chapters 3 and 4.

Something You Can Do

Complete the following steps to organize your list of sustained clients:

1. Create a list of individuals within your organization whom you believe meet the criteria for a client.

2. Then identify any of those individuals with whom you currently have a sustained relationship.

3. Next identify those with whom you would like to have a sustained relationship.

As you continue reading this book, you will be able to identify actions you can take to enhance the sustained relationships you currently have and/or to form sustained relationships with clients with whom an ongoing partnership is not evident at this time. Return to this page from time to time and list actions you can take.

1. Individuals with whom I currently have a sustained relationship.

Names of Individuals

Actions to Enhance the Relationship (Chapters 3 and 4 include possible actions)

2. Individuals with whom I would like a sustained relationship.

Names of Individuals

Actions to Form a Relationship (Chapters 3 and 4 include possible actions)

SBP Tips

There are four concepts that guide the practices of your work as an SBP:

1. The HR function can do three kinds of work: transactional, tactical, and strategic. As an SBP you need to do a very limited amount of transactional work. Tactical work, when done, should be in support of a strategic initiative. In essence, the majority of your time needs to be spent on supporting strategic opportunities and initiatives.

2. Within every organization there are four kinds of needs: business, performance, work environment, and capability needs. You add value as an SBP by identifying and helping clients to align these four needs.

3. Asking the "right" questions enables you to translate business requirements into performance requirements.

4. As an SBP, you need to determine who qualifies as your sustained clients and then work to gain access, credibility, and trust with these individuals.

Answers to Something You Can Do

Compare your answers to our responses listed below. We have provided rationale for each of our answers. In some instances we indicate why a response would not be correct. Hopefully, this rationale will add to your understanding of the four types of needs.

1. Question: We are in the process of reducing operational expenses in our service centers. Can you help us put together a communication program to help people in the centers understand why we are doing this?

Our answer: **BN, CN/S. *Rationale:*** The statement, "we are in the process of reducing operational expenses in our service centers" describes a business need. This need is measurable in a quantifiable manner and is vital to the future success of the business unit. The request to "put together a communication program" describes a capability solution because the end result is for "people in the centers to gain knowledge" about this initiative. This statement is not a performance need because there is no indication of what people in the centers are to do differently or better on the job as a result of the communication program.

2. Question: The managers in my region are skillful in the technical area. What I need to do is improve their interpersonal skills. They are not communicating with nor managing their teams in a satisfactory manner. Our answer: **PN, CN/S. *Rationale:*** Managers "are not communicating with nor managing the teams in a satisfactory manner" describes a performance need. The need is vague, but can be made more specific by asking the client questions. The need to "improve their interpersonal skills" is clearly a capability solution.

3. Question: We plan to increase revenue in the next year. We must ensure our talent recruitment and retention processes are ready as we need everyone performing in an optimal manner to reach our goal. Our answer: **BN, PN, WN/S. *Rationale:*** The statement begins with a clear identification of a business need "to increase revenue." It continues by stating a *solution* that is "to ensure our talent recruitment and retention processes are ready." This is a work environment solution (work systems and processes). The final statement that we need "everyone performing in an optimal manner" refers to a vague performance need.

4. Question: Our sales representatives are not focusing on the long-term strategic sales that we need in this business. I'd like to talk to you about a new sales incentive program that would offer greater rewards for this kind of sale. Our answer: **PN, WN/S.** *Rationale:* The statement that, "our sales representatives are not focusing on long-term strategic sales" describes the current performance of the sales representatives. This is something they are not doing on the job. The suggestion that a "new sales incentive program" may be required is a work environment solution, focusing on the incentive category. To qualify as a business need, there must be a statement regarding a business goal such as revenue, profitability, or market share. There likely is such a need, but it is not included in the statement as presented by the client; you will need to ask about the business need.

Chapter 2

The SBP Model

"Our principles are the springs of our actions."

Philip Skelton

Individuals who are in the people-functions of an organization wear many hats. Not only do they design and implement various solutions, such as training and team building, but they also manage change initiatives, lead people within the people-function, and deliver services that support strategic business goals. All of these responsibilities are challenging, but the role that is among the most ubiquitous and vague is that of Strategic Business Partner (SBP). Previously, this role has been described at a conceptual level. In this chapter, we provide specific information about the accountabilities for the SBP role. The model shown in Figure 2.1 describes the accountabilities of an SBP.

Partnerships that you build with clients are the foundation of your role as an SBP. Partnerships are rooted in credibility and trust. The client partnership enables you to identify strategic projects on which to work. Working on strategic projects can deepen your access, credibility, and trust with your client.

Figure 2.1 Strategic Business Partner Accountabilities

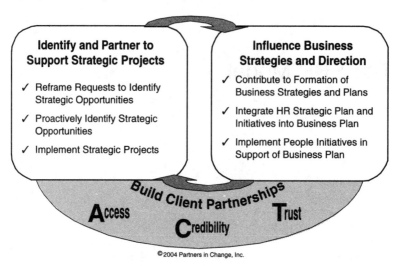

© 2004 Partners in Change, Inc.

Successful strategic projects can result in opportunities to work with business leaders, influencing strategies and directions for a business unit or the entire enterprise.

When we first began our research for this book, we viewed the three accountabilities in the SBP model as sequential. What we learned is that they are additive. As an SBP, you do not stop building partnerships as you move to the second accountability—you do both concurrently. As the accountabilities expand from a project focus to a longer-term entity focus, your job as an SBP becomes more complex and demanding. Added to this complexity is the fact that clients, with whom partnerships are formed, may transition to other jobs. New individuals come into the role, requiring the partnership building process to begin anew. After all, relationships are formed with people, not jobs. Keeping your various SBP accountabilities in balance is a true challenge.

Another insight that occurred to us is that not all SBPs will work on the accountability of "influencing business strategies and directions." For many, the building of partnerships and partnering with clients on strategic projects are the focus and provide ample opportunity to have impact and add value. Let's take a closer look at the accountabilities of an SBP.

Build Client Partnerships

In this accountability you establish strong collaborative relationships with managers who have responsibility for business units or departments within the enterprise. It is essential that you identify those specific managers with whom partnerships should be developed, at both a sustained and project level, using the criteria provided in Chapter 1. But what type of partnerships must be developed with clients who are responsible for achieving the business goals in your organization? We have found there are three key factors that are essential to successful partnerships: access, credibility and trust. Let's look at each of these in more detail.

Access

Access consists of two components: (1) determining the specific owners of the business and performance needs and (2) gaining "face time" with those individuals.

When you are first assigned to support a business unit, it is important to identify managers who are the strategic decision makers. These are the managers who are driving the business and responsible for getting results. Of course, the number of managers varies depending on the size of the business. These managers are the ones with whom you will form sustained client relationships—partnerships in which you invest time independent of any project work. Even though you may be involved in projects that originate from other managers, it is important to periodically meet, either personally or by phone, with each of your sustained clients. You want to stay current with their business requirements, challenges, and strategic initiatives. These meetings are an excellent venue to clarify your role as SBP and build credibility.

Credibility

Credibility is achieved when your clients believe in your capability to deliver results for the business. It means your clients are confident you will deliver the results they expect to the agreed-upon criteria and standards. When you have credibility, your clients know you will take actions that have a positive impact on employee's performance and the business results.

When moving into the SBP role, you want your clients to view you as a person who eagerly accepts responsibility and shared accountability for getting results. This requires a deep understanding of your client's business goals and strategies. When you are assigned to a project, you need to jump into the project with enthusiasm, eager to take on new responsibilities and to get the project moving quickly.

Credibility requires that you have a deep knowledge of the business you support. Clients want to partner with Human Resource (HR) professionals who understand the organization's business model and the external forces impacting upon the organization. So as an SBP, you need knowledge of both HR processes *and* business systems. Expertise only in HR will be insufficient to earn credibility as an SBP.

Trust

Trust is an elusive concept that is also critical to your success as an SBP. Trust is evident when your clients have confidence in your integrity and reliability to achieve results in support of the business. Developing trust requires congruence between what you say and what you do.

You have developed trust with a business leader when that person has confidence in the moral and ethical code by which you perform your job. You demonstrate this in multiple ways: by honoring the confidentiality of information and sources and by openly discussing and confronting issues of potential conflict and ethics with your clients. So it is important to be aware of potential ethical issues when taking on projects.

You also develop trust with clients when they see that the actions you take are in the best interest of the organization, evidencing respect for individuals impacted by those actions. A balanced approach toward achieving business results while also having concern for individuals is a challenge you will face.

Building partnerships with clients requires you to identify the appropriate people with whom these relationships are needed. One of the most common errors made by people in a consultative role, particularly when working on a project, is to learn too late that they are not partnered with the true client. Therefore, be thoughtful in identifying the specific individuals with whom you will develop sustained and project partnerships. Then work to build access, credibility, and trust with these individuals.

SBP Example

Who Is the "True Client"?

David, an SBP within an organization that manufactures kitchen and bath fixtures, formed a partnership with the product manager for one brand of fixtures. This product manager was responsible for designing and implementing the marketing plan for a new line of upscale fixtures. In the discussions with the product manager, David learned the details of the product launch and the needs of the sales force who would be asked to sell these fixtures. Through interviews and information obtained regarding the marketing plan, David determined three keys to ensuring support of the sales force to this product line launch. The sales force would need to be highly skilled in influencing retailers to allocate showroom and inventory space to the new product line. The marketing materials and online information for retailers and the sales force would need to be upgraded. The incentive plan for the sales force must be modified to encourage sales of the new product line, rather than continuing to sell the current products.

David put together a comprehensive proposal for addressing these needs, with the ultimate goal of gaining strong support of the sales force for the product line. The proposal was submitted to the project manager for approval. One week later David met with the product manager to discuss the proposal and the next steps to be taken. Imagine David's surprise when the product manager said, "Your proposal is a no-go." David asked, "Why not? You and I agreed that we needed a plan for getting the support of the sales force and retailers. What happened?" The product manager replied, "My boss, the VP of Marketing, did not like the plan. He thought there was an easier way to gain commitment." The key learning for David: The product manager was not the client for this initiative. The real client was the VP of Marketing. The VP was responsible for achieving the sales goal and was the ultimate decision maker. Without a relationship with him, David had little chance of developing a proposal that was aligned with the "true" client's perspective, preferences, and requirements.

Identify and Partner to Support Strategic Projects

With the development of client partnerships underway, you are in a position to identify opportunities to work on projects of significant business impact. The primary purpose of this accountability is to work on projects that directly benefit the business. The challenge is to demonstrate to clients that you can act strategically to accomplish business results, not just deliver HR and other solutions. To work strategically also means you need to operate systematically, "connecting the dots" between business requirements, performance needs, and people initiatives. If you have read our book *Performance Consulting*, this SBP accountability will sound familiar. In essence, the accountability of working with clients on strategic projects requires that you utilize a performance consulting process. This is project-based work and is key to adding value in your role as an SBP. These projects are obtained both reactively and proactively.

Reframe Requests to Identify Strategic Opportunities

As an SBP, you likely find much of your work is initiated by a client request—usually as a request to implement some type of HR or learning solution. Sometimes these requests are in support of a strategic goal; other times the requested solutions are presented as tactics with no apparent link to a goal or strategy. Perhaps you can relate to requests such as:

- "I want to discuss my plans for reorganizing the department."

- "Sales representatives are not focusing on the sales of our new product. Let's discuss modifying the sales incentive plan."

- "When can you run diversity training for my group?"

Experience shows that stand-alone projects, with limited linkage to a business goal or strategy, often fall short of the results a client expects. Therefore you want to think and act strategically and integrate business needs, performance needs, and people initiatives. You do this by reframing requests for stand-alone projects. Reframing is a process of transitioning the client and the discussion away from a focus on a solution and toward a focus on desired results. Reframing consists of acknowledging the request and then asking questions about the performance and business needs linked to that request. Reframing is done for two reasons: (1) to ensure that any solution delivered will yield results the client seeks and (2) to determine what information is currently unknown and must be obtained. Reframing enables you to direct HR resources to initiatives where impact will be the greatest.

An inherent problem with reframing a request is that the client has already decided on the solution to be taken. This brings two factors into play. First, the clients have made a decision to implement the solution—that is why they have called you. The reframing process requires the client to rethink that solution, and in some cases the client may be unwilling to do this. Second, reframing discussions are further downstream in the decision-making process than is desirable. Influencing the client at this late stage in the decision-making process is more problematic. If you utilize only the reframing technique to move into strategic work, the probabilities are that some strategic opportunities will be missed. Therefore, to be proficient as an SBP you also need to conduct proactive business needs discussions with clients.

Proactively Identify Strategic Opportunities

There are several methods you can use as an SBP to operate proactively. One of the primary methods is to *initiate* meetings with clients to discuss business needs and the implications of these needs for people's performance. There are two purposes for these discussions: (1) to deepen your knowledge of the "business of the business" and (2) to look for opportunities to support a client's business needs that would not have otherwise been identified this early. In essence, a proactive conversation is a type of marketing activity. As with reframing, proactive discussions require asking the right questions right. You not only ask about business goals, measures, and challenges but also about the employee groups that are most critical to achieving those goals and what those groups must do if the goals are to be achieved. These questions often result in a client realizing the required performance of the workgroups has not been determined. This is a great entry point for you as an SBP. Proactive discussions identify strategic work that is further upstream, providing more time to obtain valuable information that will lead to better decisions.

Even if strategic work is not identified, your proactive discussions will advance and deepen your client partnerships. You gain information about current business needs and challenges facing the manager. And you are certainly demonstrating your interest in understanding the business, which can result in future opportunities to work with that client.

Implement Strategic Projects

Both reframing and proactive business goals discussions can lead to strategic work with the client. Once clients make the decision to partner with you on this type of project, they want to move expeditiously. As one HR director said, "When the opportunity for a strategic project presents itself, grab the ball and run with it. Don't wait for permission to move ahead. Just jump into the project and get a win for the client."

So when your client says, "Yes. Let's move ahead on that project," immediately affirm the project's goals and intended outcomes with your client. This is to ensure that you and the client are marching down the same road. It is highly probable that some assessment will be required. Perhaps the need will be to determine what specific employees need to do more, better, or differently if the business goals are to be achieved. Sometimes your client already knows what employees need to do, but will need help identifying the root causes of a performance problem. Once you have identified the root causes, you and your client can discuss and agree on the solutions to be implemented. And then the *real* work begins—implementing solutions that result in enhanced performance and business impact.

When first in the role of SBP, you most likely will find that your projects are narrow in scope with limited impact upon organizational strategies. You may also be partnering with managers who are one or two levels below those accountable for achieving the business unit's goals. In these cases your objective is to work your way up the organizational ladder. To do this you need to provide the very best support on projects for the managers with whom you *are* partnered. Over a period of time, as you successfully manage these projects, your credibility will be enhanced, the scope of projects will grow, and you will be enlarging the circle of people who are your clients.

SBP Example

Identifying Strategic Opportunities by Reframing Requests

When the VP of Sales said that he wanted to meet to discuss a training need, Mark felt that it had something to do with the gross margin problem. Mark is an SBP who supports the sales division within a firm that manufactures heating and air conditioning equipment. Many of the sales are complex, requiring the sales executives to work with engineers to design the installation and compute the pricing. The two groups were not working together as well as they should; in fact, there were some real conflicts. The VP of Sales wanted the sales executives and engineers trained in team building. He felt this would result in more effective work relationships. Mark realized that he would need to reframe this request because it was doubtful team-building training by itself would solve the problem. In the meeting, Mark acknowledged the VP's request for team-building training and then asked, "What have you seen that leads you to believe the team-building training is needed?" The VP provided several examples of the failure of the sales executives and engineers to work well together, resulting in poorly designed, low profit installations. When Mark asked the VP to describe how he expected the sales executives and engineers to work together, the VP described his expectations in great detail. When asked how many sales executives and engineers were now working that way, the VP responded that none were and went on to say, "That's why they need team-building training." Mark responded that he could provide excellent team-building training, but wondered, "Would there be other barriers to the two groups working well together once they were trained?" This question prompted a discussion where both Mark and the VP acknowledged several factors that would make working together difficult, negatively impacting gross margins. The problem was that both Mark and the VP were uncertain of what factors were posing the greatest challenges to the teams. As a result of the reframing discussion, the VP saw the need to obtain more information. This information revealed multiple root causes. There was a lack of role clarity between sales executives and the engineers. Also the projects that required design of heating and air conditioning systems were randomly assigned to engineers. Therefore, the engineers and sales executives did not have opportunities to work together on multiple projects, developing knowledge of each other's work style and approach. Furthermore, the incentive system did not encourage them to spend time working together.

With this information, the VP of Sales and Mark were able to make decisions about solutions to address these causes. Although team-building training was required, there were other solutions that focused on role clarity, assignment of engineers, and incentives. The result? The sales executives and engineers worked together more as teams, developed better proposals, and increased the gross margins on their joint sales. Mark's reframing of the request for team-building training resulted in a more complete solution, achievement of the client's desired business results, and enhanced credibility for Mark as an SBP.

Influence Business Strategies and Direction

In this stage, you are participating with other business leaders in the formation of strategies to ensure organizational success. The breadth and scope of work now addresses the needs of large business units or the entire enterprise. As Lawler and Mohrman indicate, "The greatest benefits occur when Human

Resources is a strategic partner that fully participates in both the development and implementation of the 'business' strategy" (2003, p. 20). When working within this accountability, you participate in the forming of business strategies and plans for an entity or enterprise, you integrate HR strategies into these business plans, and you implement people initiatives that support the business plans. Let's look at each of these separately.

Contribute to Formation of Business Strategies and Plans

For this accountability your focus is not so much on single departments as on the organization's business units or even the entire organization itself. Therefore, the issues discussed are more complex and initially less defined. It is possible that the work done here will affect the business and its future direction for several years to come. In this role you work as a *business person* first and an HR professional second. For example, if retailing is the business, you think like a retailer; if manufacturing is the business, your deep knowledge of that business model is required.

For any business strategy to be effective, it must address the needs of the market and support the organization's business model and values while optimizing the human capital of the organization. The market needs determine what customers will buy. The business model describes how the organization will provide a product and/or service of value to the market in a financially viable manner. The performance of people within the organization will enable—or limit—the organization's success in implementing the business model. Clearly, to be helpful in forming business strategies, you need a deep understanding of the business, its strategic processes, *and* HR capability and solutions.

Using this knowledge, you will be actively engaged in strategic discussions. One way you add value as an SBP is by translating current and future business needs into requirements for the workforce. Senior executives expect you to help form the business strategy, proposing people initiatives—both HR and non-HR—required for successful execution of that strategy.

SBP Example

Contributing to Business Strategies

The issue on the table was the introduction to the market place of the company's new offering. The financial services firm had traditionally offered specific services, such as asset planning and tax preparation, to its clients. Now it had the capability of providing its clients with strategic planning, marketing analysis, and brand development. This would enable the firm to transition from generating revenue primarily from projects to revenue obtained through multiyear contracts with clients.

The Vice President for Sales had presented a plan for having all the account executives sell the multiyear contracts to current and new clients. The account executives would also continue to sell current projects to clients who were not interested in a long-term contract. Of course, the sales force would need to have a few additional account executives to handle the additional workload and increase in revenue. Keith, a Human Resource Senior Executive, acknowledged the need for the sales force to generate revenue through multiyear contracts. Keith went on to say, "My concern is that the selling process for these contracts is considerably different from that for selling projects. This new approach calls for sales people to have competency in areas that are different from our current account executive capabilities. For example, sales people, who are selling long-term contracts, must develop a relationship with several executives in the client firm, gaining their support for the contract. This is different than the process now where relationships are formed with a single individual. We are moving to a much more complex, and long-term, sale."

Keith's comments generated discussion by the six business leaders around the table. The end result was a decision to recruit a few senior account executives who possessed the new competencies. The business leaders also discussed the need for a unique compensation plan, based upon specific business goals, for these new senior account executives. Certainly, Keith was at the table, helping to influence decisions regarding a business strategy and how to ensure its success.

Integrate HR Strategic Plan and Initiatives into the Business Plan

Once the business strategies are formed, it is vital that the work of the HR function be linked into those strategies. Does a strategy require a revised organizational architecture or structure? If it does, a goal for the HR function is to support that requirement. Is there a need to more fully understand the client organization's readiness to embrace a strategy? Then the HR function can implement an organizational audit for that purpose. And what enhanced capability of people will be required? Surely the HR function needs to direct HR resources to support this requirement. When HR initiatives support business goals and strategies, the work done by people within the HR function will be of great value to the organization.

Certainly, the HR leader has the ultimate decision-making role regarding allocation of HR resources. As an SBP, you may not be in that role. Therefore, it becomes vital that you influence and guide decisions within the HR function regarding initiatives to be supported. In this way you are influencing in two directions: outside the HR function to the organization's leaders and within the HR function to its leadership.

Implement People Initiatives in Support of Business Plan

Once business strategies are formed and people initiatives are aligned with those strategies, you as an SBP have a primary responsibility to implement the "people" portion of the business plan. You may have noticed our use of the term *people initiatives*. This is the term we prefer to use when discussing any initiative designed to enhance performance of people. These initiatives frequently, but not exclusively, emanate from the HR function. To implement the people initiatives successfully, you need strong project management skills, including the skill of selecting the right people to manage the day-to-day activities. You will most likely work as an orchestrator of resources. You will not personally implement many of the people solutions but rather will delegate that responsibility to others. Additionally, you need to anticipate problems and identify weaknesses in the HR plan early on so that those issues can be addressed. The best tactic for managing barriers is to prevent them from occurring. There is a saying that good pilots fly 15 minutes ahead of the aircraft. Correspondingly, good SBPs are aware of what may happen 30 days ahead of project mileposts.

It is critical that you assume some of the accountability for successful execution of business strategies. Partnership ultimately means shared accountability. The implication is that as an SBP, you are concerned with the rollout of the entire strategy and not just the portion for which you are personally responsible. As one HR executive said, "The SBP must think like a CEO and monitor each business strategy as it is rolled out." When any part of the business strategy is faltering, the whole strategy is in jeopardy. Lawler and Mohrman state that, "Most strategies, like most mergers, fail not because of poor thinking, but because of poor implementation" (2003, p. 2). This being the case, as an SBP you have both a responsibility and an opportunity to support business leaders and initiatives during their implementation.

You evidence this shared accountability when you monitor how employees, supervisors, and managers are accepting and reacting to the business strategy being implemented. You need to actively seek feedback by asking such questions as, "What changes are taking place because of this strategy?" and "What concerns do people have regarding this change?"

By seeking feedback from several levels in the organization— employees, supervisors, and managers—you obtain a picture of the progress of the implementation and its acceptance by employees. This is vital information about the implementation of strategies you can share with business leaders. Effective business leaders use this type of information to make midcourse adjustments during implementation.

As an SBP, you have the opportunity to provide a unique perspective. Because of your in-depth knowledge of how and why people may choose to support or resist a new strategy, you can guide the change process. It is vital that you combine this expertise with feedback from employees in a way that increases the probability of success for each business strategy implemented.

Something You Can Do

We have introduced you to the SBP accountabilities. In the following chapters each of these accountabilities will be described in more detail. Why not take a few minutes now to determine your current state of readiness relative to the SBP accountabilities? This will clarify where you may want to focus your reading of other chapters in this book.

1. *Build Client Partnerships.* To what degree have you developed strategic, business-linked partnerships with clients in your organization? Is this accountability fully developed or is it an area where you want to develop more?
   Write your answers here:_____
   _____
   _____

   Chapters 3 and 4 of this book will provide more content and suggested practices for building these partnerships.

2. *Identify and Partner on Strategic Projects.* How many strategic projects have you supported in the last year? Is this an area where you might want to be spending more time? And are the projects you work on identified primarily in a reactive or proactive manner?
Write your answers here: _____

_____

_____

Chapters 5, 6, 7, and 8 will provide you with ideas on identifying and supporting strategic initiatives.

3. *Influence Business Strategies and Direction.* This is the accountability that truly places you "at the table" with the leaders of your organization. Is this something you are doing now? Is it a goal to which you aspire?
Write your answers here:_____

_____

_____

Chapter 9 focuses on some of the key "how-to's" for this accountability.

SBP Tips

In your role as an SBP, you have three major accountabilities. Each accountability builds upon the others and increases in complexity. The three SBP accountabilities are:

1. *Build Client Partnerships.* This requires access, credibility, and trust. To build partnerships you must have face-to-face time with your clients. In addition you must develop credibility, where your clients believe that you can deliver results for the business. And the third element of the partnership is trust, where clients have confidence in your integrity and reliability to achieve results for the business.

2. *Identify and Partner to Support Strategic Projects.* This accountability consists of proactively and reactively identifying substantive projects to work on with clients. When you and your client agree on a strategic project, you need to jump into the project and quickly assess the situation. This accountability also includes identifying and helping to implement the many people initiatives required to ensure a success for the business.

3. *Influence Business Strategies and Direction.* Here you are working with business leaders to shape the future of the organization. Together you are scanning the horizon for opportunities as well as monitoring the organization for problems. Through open discussion and debate, the management team agrees on strategies, goals, and actions. These become the business plan. Working as a link between the HR function and the business leaders, you engage the HR leadership team in developing HR strategies and plans that align with and support the business plan. Then you work to ensure flawless execution of the people initiatives required. Monitoring the implementation and providing updates to the leaders is also a key role for you as an SBP.

PART TWO

BUILDING CLIENT PARTNERSHIPS

Figure P2.1 Strategic Business Partner Accountabilities

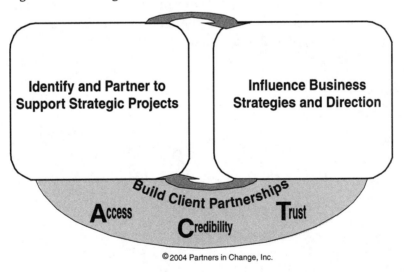

The relationships developed with clients are the foundation for work as a Strategic Business Partner (SBP). There are three elements required to build and maintain ongoing partnerships with managers and leaders:

- *Access* to those individuals who have accountability for achieving business results within the organization. It is not possible to partner with someone when there is no direct contact. But how do you decide with whom you should form partnerships? In these chapters we provide criteria for determining who should be your clients as well as practices for gaining and maintaining access to these individuals.

- *Credibility* with clients, so that they have confidence you will deliver as promised. Earning credibility is directly related to the depth of knowledge you have of both Human Resource (HR) processes *and* the "business of the business." But how do you learn the workings of the business when you are first assigned to a business unit? Techniques to learn the business model and operations are discussed here.

- *Trust* that you can be relied upon to deliver results, working with integrity and in support of the organization's values. Trust is developed over a long period of time. However, it can be lost in the blink of an eye. The techniques to use and to avoid are described here.

Chapter 3

Identifying Clients and Developing Access

"If senior management sees me only when there is a problem, that is how they will think of me."

Strategic Business Partner

Strategic Business Partners (SBPs) can play an important role in developing and implementing business strategies. But they can not do this by themselves—they are not lone rangers. Rather, SBPs must have a strong partnering relationship with management, a relationship that is the foundation for strategic work. Partnering with management is required to gain insight into business needs and the challenges faced by employees who must achieve those business goals. This insight enables SBPs to assist management in translating business goals into performance requirements, removing barriers, and making other needed changes.

In Chapter 1 we described our criteria for identifying clients. We also indicated that there are two categories of clients: sustained and project. In Chapter 2 we indicated that the first accountability of SBPs is to "develop partnerships built upon access, credibility, and trust," captured in the acronym A-C-T. Let's look more deeply at how you gain access to clients.

Gaining Access to Sustained Clients

Gaining access to a new sustained client can be challenging. However, without access to the client, there is no way you can be involved in strategic work. As one SBP indicated, "If I am going to get a win, I have to be on the team."

Access means you have quality and quantity "face time" with the leader. Organizations use a variety of terms to refer to the leaders they support. Some use the term *client;* others use *sponsors, customers, partners,* or *client teams.* Although the term may vary from one organization to another, the criteria used to identify these individuals does not. As noted in Chapter 1, sustained clients own business needs and are people with whom you should form a relationship independent of project work.

There are three steps to take when working to gain access to sustained clients.

The first step is to identify individuals in the business unit who should become sustained clients, taking actions so you are known to these individuals. Using the criteria noted and gathering reliable information about the business unit will help identify those individuals who should be your sustained clients. Typically, a single SBP builds relationships with between five and ten sustained clients. These are the people with whom substantive time will be spent during the course of a year. We encourage you to work from the concept that "less is more." It is not possible to build a partnering relationship, spending the required time, with 30 or 40 individuals. This is one reason why most SBPs are assigned to support one or more business units and not the entire enterprise. The exception would be if you work in a small company, where supporting the entire organization is possible to do.

So how do you get started? When assigned to a new business unit, first review the organization chart and identify those people who have the position power to make things happen and have accountability for achieving business results. Next learn more about the business unit, going below the organization chart to gain insight regarding items such as:

- How are important decisions made within the business unit? Is a collaborative and consensus-seeking process used? A more unilateral process?

- Who is at the table when strategic direction and goals are being determined?

- What recent initiatives have enabled the organization to be successful?

- Who were the key players in deciding and implementing those initiatives?

- Who has the power of veto on strategic decisions?

Answers to these questions can provide insight as to which leaders are driving the business and have the power to get things done. You want to be working with these individuals because they have the most to gain or lose from the success or failure of a strategic initiative. As one SBP said, "When identifying clients, you go as high as you can (within the chain of command)." A word of caution, however; relationships are made with people, not jobs. When a client is promoted or leaves the job for any reason, and a new person steps in, you must build the relationship all over again.

Once you have identified those individuals with whom you should have a sustained relationship, it becomes important to find ways to gain access to them. You want to be on their radar screen, so that when there is a strategic opportunity they will think of including you right from the start. It is possible you already have a relationship with some—perhaps all—of these individuals. But first ask yourself, "Is this a relationship primarily based upon providing solutions in a tactical manner or is it truly a strategic, business-linked partnership?" Different tactics are required when your goal is to become known to a potential client versus when your goal is to transition from a tactical to a strategic relationship. In Table 3.1 we provide some suggested actions to take if you lack access with a person who should be a sustained client. In Table 3.2 are suggested actions for transitioning a relationship from a tactical to a strategic focus.

Table 3.1
Actions for Gaining Access to Clients with Whom You Have Limited/No Access

- Initiate contact with the client by asking for time to discuss business goals and challenges that the client is facing (NOTE: Chapter 7 provides an interview guide that you can use for this purpose.)
- Send articles from journals and industry magazines that focus on items of importance to this client's business. Include a note indicating why you believe the item has relevance for the client.
- Initiate contact with the client, indicating you would like to learn more about the client's business. Ask the client how you can increase your knowledge of the business. In essence, ask your client to become your coach.
- Volunteer to serve on high-visibility projects and task teams that are important to this client.
- When in meetings with the client and others, ask questions that expand the thinking and discussion of the group.
- Leverage current relationships with other managers to assist you in gaining access to the client.
- Publicize your "wins." Ask your clients, with whom you work, to market the results to their peers.

Table 3.2
Actions for Transitioning a Sustained Client from a Tactical to Strategic Relationship

---

- Be alert to information from various parts of the organization that has impact upon your client's business unit. Send this information to your client, indicating that you would like to discuss the implications of this with your client.
  "Essentially I indicate that I am hearing some things from Operations that could have implications for what we are doing in Sales, and I would like to discuss these implications with the client."
- Ask to attend the client's staff meetings as an observer, so you gain greater insights into the business. When in these meetings, expand thinking of the group by asking thought-provoking questions.
- Provide guidance to the client during a crisis.
  "The results from an opinion survey were very distressing to my client, so I offered suggestions that might be used to close the gaps."
- In discussions, keep focus on the business results that are needed rather than on the tactics to be implemented. Help clients to avoid the "jump to solution" approach.
- Offer suggestions about how you can help on a project or business situations in which you are currently involved.
  "On the redesign project, I indicated how I could help with the work flow analysis; I had worked on a similar project at a different site."

SBP Example

Gaining Access through Coaching Leaders

Diane was newly assigned as an SBP to support the Operations group within her organization. She identified those leaders with whom a sustained relationship was not yet developed, but was needed. She was known to some of these individuals, but not to all. She did not have a strong partnership with any of them.

It so happened that the organization had just concluded a major climate assessment. The plan was to have the leaders in each major area share the findings with both their direct and indirect reporting employees. Diane saw an opportunity to gain access to these leaders by volunteering to be their coach through this process. She

became involved in forming their Microsoft PowerPoint®
presentations, observed the leaders as they did "dry runs"
of their presentations, sat through the presentations, and
debriefed with them after their meetings with employees.
Through this process Diane was viewed as a partner who
added value. One leader said, "You helped me see the
survey results through the eyes of the employees. That
made all the difference in the world." Another leader com-
mented, "You understood that I was uncomfortable with
these meetings with employees. Your coaching and feedback during the dry runs convinced me that I could handle the meetings." She also came to learn much more
about the operations area, its business goals and challenges. When the project had concluded, Diane had not
only developed access, but had gained credibility and
trust with these leaders. Her sustained client relationships
were well positioned for the future.

*The second step is to prepare yourself and your department to support
the strategic initiatives that will eventually come your way.* You do
this by concentrating on three fundamental underpinnings:

- Learn the business of the business units you support. In
  the next chapter we discuss many tactics you can use to
  develop this knowledge. Suffice to say now it is vital to
  have a thorough understanding of the business model
  and why it works for this business unit. You need to
  know how each job within the business unit supports
  this business model, including the goals and strategies
  that support the model. How is the business unit structured? What are the strengths and vulnerabilities of
  that structure? Many SBPs who are new to a business
  unit spend time in the plants or with the sales force,
  working along side the people at those locations for a
  day or two. The SBPs gain insight regarding those jobs
  and also find out what's working and not working for
  people on the frontline.

- As you learn about the business of the business, reshape your role by asking questions that expand people's thinking. You can ask about the alignment of the four needs in the hierarchy, increasing client awareness about the degree to which there is, or is not, alignment. You can observe workplace problems, indicating how you can add value in resolving these problems. Describe to others how to optimize you and your role for the benefit of the organization. This shaping of your role enables you to respond effectively and rapidly when strategic initiatives are identified. Additionally, you can share your knowledge of the business with others in the HR area, further ensuring alignment of HR with the business.

- Be responsive to all requests from clients. Manage requests, no matter how small, in a professional manner. Make sure you have a clear understanding of the clients' needs and deliver more than they expect. By responding promptly and providing the client with excellent service, you are demonstrating that you and the HR function can be relied upon to support the business unit.

The third step is to hit the ground running when given an opportunity to partner on a major initiative. Many SBPs with whom we have worked indicate that the tipping point began when they were asked by a new client to take on a major responsibility within a highly visible initiative. These SBPs discovered they were now working with a client who had a lot to gain or lose from the success or failure of the project.

Should you receive this type of opportunity, the key is to move fast. Clarify the scope of the project with your client. Reach agreement with the client on the key metrics by which the project would be measured. Discuss the challenges to be faced and potential problems that could derail the project. At the same time, put a plan together to organize resources so that the project work can be launched quickly.

In many cases a member of the client team chairs the task force; as an SBP your role is as a member of that task force. Each member of the task force has substantial accountability for the project's success. To get a win, you need to initiate actions on your own, acquiring both resources and cooperation of others. In all cases your actions will directly impact upon the project's results. Project success is vital to clients, to the organization, and to you. How you work with your clients and other project team members is as important as the results achieved. The key learning? Getting a win and doing it with style leads to a stronger partnership with the client.

SBP Example

Jumping on Strategic Opportunities

Judith worked in a professional services organization that was merging with another organization. After the merger she continued to work in the role of HR Manager, supporting her original company that was now a division of the newly formed organization. In this role she took actions to develop a solid working knowledge of the larger organization's business model. After approximately a year, a line manager, whom she supported, offered her a new position. The line manager was being promoted to head a new division resulting from yet another merger. The employees in this division were having difficulty assimilating into the organization. For the next several months, Judith spent much of her time in the field offices of the division, working with and talking to employees in numerous locations. She obtained in-depth knowledge of the problems being faced by the field offices. Judith provided her client with information about those problems. She helped division management focus attention on the systems that needed improvement. She worked with field offices to clarify accountabilities and implement best practices required for goal achievement. During this time she learned that many managers, supervisors, and employees distrusted the division management team. Many felt that upper management did not care about their concerns and were very autocratic.

Without being asked, Judith provided her client with information about the discontent she was hearing. She indicated, "As I listen to people at all levels in the division, I hear them saying that division leadership does not care about them—that you will cut jobs just to make the numbers—that division leaders are autocratic and hard to reach."

Her client, somewhat surprised, asked Judith for more specifics. He then asked what she felt he and his team could do to turn things around. Judith suggested that the leadership team spend more time in the field being accessible to employees, seeking and responding to questions and concerns. In addition, Judith encouraged her client to be more visible and to communicate his vision of a bright future for the division. The division head discussed this information with his team. They agreed that quick and decisive action was required. They moved quickly to implement Judith's recommendations. After six months the morale of the employees started to turn around. People began to believe that the division would be successful and that leadership viewed the employees as a critical component for success.

By helping her client get a win out of this difficult situation, Judith demonstrated she could make things happen. By taking the initiative to advise her client, she helped the project become more successful and increased her credibility with her client and the management team.

Gaining Access to the Project Client

Let's now look at how gaining access to project clients differs from gaining access to sustained clients. Certainly, a major difference is that your level of contact with a project client is only intense during the life of the project. What is the same are the criteria used to determine the true client for the project. Project clients own the business results supported by the initiative. Unfortunately, often the person who initially calls regarding a project does not meet the client criteria. This person or "contact" has been delegated the responsibility for the activities within a specific project. The ultimate accountability for the project's results, however, reside with someone else who is the true client.

Without direct access to the true client, it will be difficult for you to influence and guide the project implementation strategy. To gain access to the true client without alienating the contact requires that you work with—not around—the contact. For example, when there are questions about the business goals, suggest that you and the contact meet together with the client to discuss these issues. When the contact lacks authority or power to obtain resources, suggest that you and the contact go together to present the situation to the true client. When you have good relations with the contact, it becomes possible to be candid and direct, indicating concern about the limited access to and involvement of the true client. Bottom line: it is important to gain access to the true client for any project where the end goal is to effect a change in people's performance and positively impact business results.

Something You Can Do

1. List up to three individuals with whom you believe you *should* partner on a sustained basis. You may want to refer to names you identified in the *Something You Can Do* exercise in Chapter 1.

   a.

   b.

   c.

2. What is your partnering relationship with these individuals? Fill in the name of each individual and assess the relationship on the scale provided.

Name

a. _____

Current Level of Relationship with this Person is:

1	2	3	4
Non-Existent	I have access but limited partnering opportunities	I have access, partnering primarily on tactical projects and requests	I have access, partnering on both strategic and tactical projects

b. _____

Current Level of Relationship with this Person is:

1	2	3	4
Non-Existent	I have access but limited partnering opportunities	I have access, partnering primarily on tactical projects and requests	I have access, partnering on both strategic and tactical projects

c. _____

Current Level of Relationship with this Person is:

1	2	3	4
Non-Existent	I have access but limited partnering opportunities	I have access, partnering primarily on tactical projects and requests	I have access, partnering on both strategic and tactical projects

3. Are there any individuals with whom the assessment is a 1? If so, you may want to refer to Table 3.1 for ideas on how to gain access to these individuals.

4. Are there individuals on your list with whom you have access but the current relationship is rated as a 2 or 3? This is an opportunity to transition the relationship from tactical to strategic. Refer to Table 3.2 for some ideas on how to do this.

Readiness Factors for Gaining Access

Gaining access to leaders who become sustained clients is an SBP accountability. But this accountability is made easier when the organization in which you work is supportive of this effort. There are three factors over which clients have tremendous influence and are critical to establishing a partnering relationship. Let's look at each of these.

1. Organizational Culture and Norms

Value for Both Collaboration and Individual Accountability. In a favorable culture the CEO or business head stresses the need for a balance between collaboration and individual accountability. To do this the leader clarifies expectations for what is to be accomplished (the results), who is ultimately responsible (the accountability), and how it is to be done (in a collaborative, inclusive manner). The emphasis on achieving results and collaborating with others establishes a climate that is favorable to strategic business partnering.

Easy access to information and people. A climate supporting ease of access to relevant business information is important. The culture should encourage open communication and information sharing rather than limit access to only "certain" people. To work strategically you need access to information regarding the goals, results, business plans, challenges, and vulnerabilities of departments and business units. This enables you to make decisions that support a department's goals while not having negative impact upon other departments. In addition, it is essential that you have access to any individual within the business units and departments you support. This access facilitates discussions regarding ideas, strategies, and concerns as they relate to the business unit. Moving freely throughout the business unit and discussing important topics with key individuals provide a favorable climate for strategic business partnering.

Inclusion in decision making. A third cultural element to consider is the decision-making process. How inclusive is it? Ideally, the business unit head encourages others to provide input and suggestions regarding business goals and strategies. When factors are making it difficult to achieve business goals, seeking input from others provides a wealth of information. No good idea will be overlooked! This climate encourages you to come forth with ideas and suggestions. It encourages a synergistic dialogue with individuals in the business unit. The results: an examination of pros and cons of all alternatives before the final strategic decision is made and a feeling of ownership for the goals and strategies selected.

2. The Direct Manager's Impact

In addition to the organization's culture, we have learned that the direct manager of an SBP has tremendous impact upon the ease or difficulty by which the SBP gains access to clients. Certainly this finding should not surprise anyone. Generally, the SBP's direct manager is not a client; rather, this manager is a formal leader who can take actions to either enable or obstruct access to business clients.

Awareness of strategic role. The direct HR manager requires a clear understanding of the economic and competitive factors impacting upon the business of the enterprise. This manager needs knowledge of the organization's business plan and the implications of these plans for talent management. The aware HR manager views employees as a competitive advantage and knows HR can play a key role in maximizing employee contribution and capability. An HR manager supportive of the SBP role wants to transition from a traditional function into one that partners with business leaders and addresses strategic issues. This manager will strive to find alternative methods for managing transactional issues, which provides time to increase efforts and effectiveness in addressing strategic issues.

Facilitating SBP visibility. Effective HR managers help new SBPs gain visibility and access to the organization's leaders. These managers often assign new SBPs to task teams and projects where the SBPs have contact with the organization's leaders. It is important that the HR manager not only provide visibility but also ensure SBPs understand the business issues to be discussed. HR managers can coach and provide candid feedback to the SBPs. This coaching and feedback increases the probability that the SBP will be successful in whatever situation is presented.

3. Organizational Pain

Another factor that can increase access to key leaders is organizational pain. When in pain, business leaders are receptive to support from an SBP. In one situation we worked in, the source of pain was the management team's late realization that they were in a changing market and needed a new brand strategy. In another situation the organization was considerably below its profit goal, despite significant investments to turn the situation around. No matter the reason, whenever the organization is under this type of stress, senior leaders are more open to enlisting the help of SBPs who truly understand the "business of the business" and want to help.

Why Is Readiness Important?

You may ask, "Why is readiness for access important to me? I can't do anything about these readiness factors in my organization. I have to play the hand that I was dealt!" Readiness is important because without it, your chances of forming a partnership with those who should be your clients are slim. And without a client partnership, you cannot be a successful SBP. A successful consultant once told us that "a positive relationship with clients is my most important asset."

Determining your organization's readiness for access will enable you to develop a strategy for becoming a valued business partner with your clients. If you see that the organization's culture is not supportive, you may determine that your approach will be to initially get some small wins and gradually work your way up the "food chain" to sustained clients. If you see that your direct manager is not providing you with opportunities for visibility, you may need to coach your manager. In all cases your awareness of the organization's readiness will help you develop a strategy for gaining access.

Barriers to Gaining Access to Clients

Thus far we have discussed best practices for obtaining access to sustained and project clients. We have also discussed the organization and direct manager factors that facilitate this access. But there are often barriers to obtaining access. Table 3.3 provides the most common barriers that we have observed, along with suggested actions to take when experiencing any of these obstacles.

Table 3.3
Barriers to Gaining Access to Clients

Barriers	*Possible Actions to Overcome Barriers*
1. Another person in HR feels that the manager is "my client."	• Engage HR leadership and the individual in discussions about who is accountable for the sustained partnerships with the leaders of the business unit. Generally, only one person from an HR function can own a client relationship at the *sustained* level.
2. A manager who should be a sustained client is not providing you with access.	• Volunteer for presentations, projects, and task forces that will give you visibility with the manager while supporting him or her at the same time.
3. The client does not see you in an SBP role.	• Set up a meeting with the client to discuss the business unit goals and your role as an SBP.
	• Approach the client about a business unit need where you could be supportive. Do not discuss the SBP role. Just do it!
4. The manager with whom you are working is not the real client for the project. You are working with the contact, not the client.	• Ask who must approve decisions and provide resources for the initiative's success. If another manager is identified, enlist your contact's help in gaining the involvement of the true client as a member of the client team.

continued

Table 3.3
Continued

Barriers	*Possible Actions to Overcome Barriers*
5. Historically, the HR function has been primarily administrative. Value for, and resources allocated to, strategic work are minimal.	• Build value for making a change. • Engage HR leadership in discussions about the mission of HR. • Provide HR leaders with information about the changing role of HR. Suggestion: Go with your leader to a conference where the strategic role of HR is to be discussed.

Something You Can Do

Certainly the climate of the organization, the style of the CEO/business unit head, and the support of your own manager have tremendous impact upon the ease or difficulty with which you gain access. Each of these factors can vary from being helpful to being a barrier. You can form a more effective strategy if you know what factors to consider. The following exercise is designed to help you assess those factors that can have an impact upon how easy or difficult it will be for you to gain access to clients. Indicate your level of agreement regarding each of the factors, as they relate to your organization, using the scale on the following page.

Strongly Disagree	Disagree	Somewhat Disagree	Somewhat Agree	Agree	Strongly Agree
1	2	3	4	5	6

The culture of my organization:

1. Encourages clarity of goals and strategies.	1	2	3	4	5	6
2. Promotes collaboration as a way to accomplish goals.	1	2	3	4	5	6
3. Holds individuals accountable for results.	1	2	3	4	5	6
4. Encourages access to information about the business unit goals, strategies, and results.	1	2	3	4	5	6

Key managers and leaders in my organization:

5 Are accessible to me for purposes of discussing business issues and goals.	1	2	3	4	5	6
6. Encourage input and suggestions from others, in and out of the business unit, regarding strategic goals and strategies.	1	2	3	4	5	6

My manager:

1. Values a strategic role for HR.	1	2	3	4	5	6
2. Seeks to align human performance with business goals.	1	2	3	4	5	6
3. Provides me with opportunities for visibility with senior management.	1	2	3	4	5	6
4. Coaches me on how to manage new and different situations.	1	2	3	4	5	6
5. Provides me with helpful feedback on how I have handled situations.	1	2	3	4	5	6

Analysis

Once you have made your ratings, analyze the results. Look at the pattern of your ratings. The factors with ratings of 4, 5, or 6 will help you gain access to your clients; these are your enablers. Factors with ratings of 1, 2, or 3 will hinder your efforts to gain access; these are barriers to success.

1. Which of the factors will make it easier for you to gain access to clients? How can you leverage those factors to gain access to clients?

2. Which factors will make it difficult for you to gain access to clients? What work-arounds or tactics can you use to either minimize their effect or remove them altogether?

SBP Tips

1. Gaining access is the first step toward building strategic partnerships with clients. Gaining access means that you first identify those individuals with whom a strategic, sustained partnership is important and then use techniques and approaches that result in "face time" with these individuals.

2. To increase your chances of gaining access to sustained clients, assess your organization's readiness for access. Use the information from your assessment to develop a plan for gaining access to those leaders who need to be your sustained clients.

3. When working on projects, it is important to ensure that the true client for the project is engaged. This may mean influencing your contact to work with you to obtain the true client's involvement.

4. Gaining access requires a bias to action so that, when the client says yes, you respond quickly and effectively. Gaining access is not an inherent right to the role of SBP. Rather, it is earned as you demonstrate interest and commitment to work with the client for purposes of achieving business results.

Chapter 4

Gaining Credibility and Trust

"My clients refer other members of the executive team to me."

HR Business Partner

To paraphrase an old expression, "Credibility and trust are gained the old-fashioned way . . . you earn them!" These are not entitlements inherent to your role as a Strategic Business Partner (SBP). You earn them over time in an iterative manner through a collective set of behaviors and practices. You can lose credibility and trust in the same manner. Generally, a single action will not result in you losing credibility and trust; however, a pattern of inappropriate action can result in their loss. And once you lose credibility and trust, they are most difficult to regain.

Let's begin by defining how we use these two terms. *Credibility* is the confidence that others have in your capability to deliver results in support of the business. *Trust* is the confidence that others have in your integrity and reliability to achieve results in support of the business. Of these two, trust is the more personal and intangible. It links to feelings of vulnerability, affirmation, and risk associated with sharing information and accountability with another individual. We find that it is possible for people to earn credibility (in other words, to be viewed as capable) while not earning trust. It is very difficult for the reverse to be true. Generally, however, these two characteristics are developed in a related and integrated manner.

Frequently, we use the phrase, "Deliver results, not only solutions." Solutions are the actions and activities of Human Resources (HR); they are what HR professionals do. Delivering learning programs, filling open positions, and building compensation systems are examples. Results are the operational and performance impact that occurs because the solutions were effectively implemented. It is not just important that people learned but that they use the enhanced skill to perform more effectively on the job. It is not only important to have a good compensation system; this system must drive needed performance and provide a positive return on investment (ROI) to the business. Delivering results builds confidence of your clients that you can be depended upon to produce outcomes—not just services and activities.

Developing Credibility

Capability to perform is integral to credibility. As an SBP you actually require two major capabilities: deep knowledge of the business *and* expertise in HR technology, processes, and solutions. As Figure 4.1 illustrates, you add value to an organization and its leaders by linking these two major areas. You are in a unique position to view the organization laterally, identifying ways to link business and people strategies across the organization. Such integration facilitates achievement of operational and strategic goals and requires that you work as a dot-connector or integrator. Let's begin by discussing the knowledge you need regarding the business.

Figure 4.1 The SBP as an Integrator

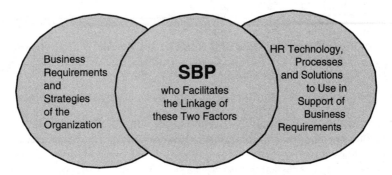

Business Knowledge

Successful SBPs are those who *think* like a business person. They essentially are business people who happen to specialize in the human side of business rather than in finance, marketing, sales, or operations. Jerold Tucker, when in his role as education director at GTE, put it this way, "If you want to bring something to the party when meeting with managers, you have to understand the financial and marketing language that they deal with every day. Once you begin talking their language, then you can begin establishing some joint partnerships" (Steinburg, 1991, p. 30).

Business knowledge is actually two-fold: knowledge of the specific organization you support and knowledge of the industry in which your organization operates. We are using the term *business knowledge* in an all-encompassing manner, referring to for-profit, not-for-profit, and public organizations. Whatever the mission of the organization, there is a business model under which it operates. As an SBP, you should know the fundamental concepts that are the underpinning of your organization's business model. You need to recognize external factors that can effect the business model positively or negatively. You want to be aware of how factors within the organization impact upon business results. How do you learn about the business model? Table 4.1 provides a list of the types of information you need to know and understand about the organization(s) you support.

Table 4.1
Business Information SBPs Need to Know and Understand

Knowledge about the Specific Organization You Support

- The business model for the organization. How are revenue and profits generated? How does the organization provide value to its customers?
- Operational metrics that are used to measure the health of the organization, including the goals and actual results. Some of the most commonly used metrics are revenue, return on assets, gross margin, market share, customer satisfaction, cost of sales, and cost of production.
- The balance sheet for your organization, indicating assets, liabilities, and equity.
- The strategic plans and initiatives implemented to support the organization's goals and requirements. Also key is knowledge of the strategic planning process used by your leaders.
- Core processes that are used to fulfill the organization's mission and achieve the results needed (i.e., order fulfillment process, sales and marketing process).
- The values and cultural norms that are not only stated but supported through behavior.
- Profile of the customers for the organization's products and services.
- Level of maturity of the business and its products/services. Is it an organization with cutting-edge products, or are products mature? Is the market just forming or commoditized?
- Primary competitors and the various competitive pressures that the organization is facing.

Knowledge about the Industry Your Organization Supports

- The marketplace within which your organization competes.
- Organizations that are the key players in this market.
- The differentiators of your organization from others in the same industry.
- Forces and factors that are impacting upon your marketplace. These are factors that are outside the control of your organization but can challenge success.
- Governmental regulatory requirements of the countries in which your organization has presence.
- The primary market segments that are sources for current and future customers for your industry and organization.
- The financial and nonfinancial benchmarks for organizations in the industry that are/can be used for comparison.
- Global factors that impact upon the industry.

We are often asked by people in HR, "How do I get this business savvy? Should I plan to get an MBA?" Although going back to a university to study business is an option, it is not a requirement and is certainly not the only option available. One option increasingly discussed is for career-HR people to rotate into a line position. Working in an operations, sales, marketing, or other role with accountability for managing a budget, and possibly profit and loss, is an excellent way to learn the "business of the business." Unfortunately, rotation to a line position is not widely embraced by HR professionals. Dr. Ed Lawler completed a study of HR functions in 150 companies and found rotation programs were among the least-used developmental tools (*Creating a Strategic Human Resources Organization,* 2003, p. 27). This is an effective approach that appears to be underutilized; we hope this changes in the coming years.

There are other ways to develop knowledge of the business and industry in which you work. Consider the following:

- Subscribe to and read on a regular basis industry journals and newsletters.

- Identify Web sites that are sources of preferred information for the leaders in your organization. Put these sites on your favorites list and visit them frequently. These will include Web sites relevant to the industry in which your organization operates.

- Arrange to have meetings with leaders in your organization. In the meeting ask questions to probe more deeply about the business. (We will discuss this tactic in detail in Chapter 7.)

- Identify people who are working in jobs for the business(es) you are supporting. Invite yourself to shadow one or more of these individuals for several hours or a day. You learn not just what they do but how the job connects to others.

You will also gain insight into the forces, factors, and opportunities that reside within the specific job and the business as a whole.

- Read annual reports and other organizational documents that provide information about the vision, mission, and strategic goals as well as about business and financial performance. Make reviewing of business plans, marketing plans, research-and-development white papers, customer service reports, and operating statements a routine practice.

- Volunteer to serve on task forces or committees that are formed to address a specific need or initiative. This will put you in touch with line and staff leaders (great for relationship-building purposes!) and also provide you with information that will deepen your knowledge of the business. This information is generally shared both within the formal agenda of group meetings as well as during informal discussions that occur through the process of working together.

- In some businesses it is possible to actually *work* the job of people you are supporting. You can learn a great deal in the process. On a few occasions each year the chief learning officer of a fast-food restaurant chain spends one day "working the line"—taking orders, and serving customers. He finds this a helpful way to stay close to his organization's customers as well as to more personally identify the evolving skill sets required of employees who work this role every day.

- If your organization employs consulting firms, seek out these consultants and pick their brains regarding what trends and issues they see occurring within the industry.

- For people who are *external consultants*, we have found the information you can obtain from an organization's Web site a good source of information about the specific business. Also, subscriber services that provide in-depth information about companies can be a valuable resource. One example of this type of service is Hoover's Online.

Clearly, there are many ways for you to develop knowledge of the "business of the business." Your credibility as an SBP is strongly correlated with the degree of business knowledge that you evidence. This knowledge is not only nice to have, it is a prerequisite to building strong partnerships with clients.

HR Knowledge

In addition to in-depth knowledge of the business, you must be an expert in the "HR function's toolkit," as Ulrich and Beatty refer to it (2001, p. 293). In their study entitled *HR as a Strategic Partner: What Does It Take to Make It Happen?*, Lawler and Mohrman report that in the hopes of positioning the HR function to operate in a more business-linked and strategic manner, some organizations have selected a non-HR executive to head the HR function. The expectation is that this will result in greater integration of HR into the business strategy and requirements. The results of the study, however, indicate that the HR function is "more likely to be a strategic partner when the head of HR has an HR background" (*HR as a Strategic Partner: What Does It Take to Make It Happen?*, 2003, p. 14). In reality, simply knowing the business is not sufficient to gain acceptance as an SBP. And, as Lawler and Mohrman acknowledge, the HR field is growing increasingly complex. Learning the field is not a simple task!

So, what must you know about HR? In Chapter 10 of this book, we provide a list of competencies you'll want to have. For now, we will focus on the knowledge of HR that you need to possess in order to gain credibility with your clients.

The foundational need is a working knowledge of multiple HR solutions, such as talent recruitment, selection, development and retention, career management, succession planning, and compensation. By *working knowledge* we mean the competence to identify opportunities where specific HR solutions would be appropriate, as well as to know when their use would be ineffective. Included in this knowledge is the capability to determine, at a macro level, the requirements for the design of the solution as well as any issues to address when implementing the HR solution. What you do *not* need is the in-depth expertise required to actually design the solution. Rarely do SBPs actually develop and implement the solutions needed for the myriad of initiatives worked upon. It would be virtually impossible to be an expert in all HR solutions that might be required. What you must have is sufficient knowledge to manage the project wisely as well as to identify and locate appropriate resources when needed.

We refer to this level of HR knowledge as a *foundational competence;* it gets you in the door. There are many other areas of HR expertise that are also required. They include:

- *Change Management.* Change is here to stay and with increasing velocity. You can provide clients with valuable guidance regarding the introduction and execution of change.

- *Consulting Model and Skills.* As an SBP you do not gain acceptance for an idea through position power; rather you gain acceptance of ideas by influencing and guiding others. This requires that you form and utilize a consulting model proven to be effective. In our opinion, SBPs must hone their consulting skills to a fine art.

- *eHR Systems.* As an SBP, you need to have a working knowledge of electronic systems and technology that are available and could be used in your organization. Certainly there are many human resource information systems (HRIS) that provide employees with access to information that facilitates decision-making regarding careers as well as management of personal benefits. This technology is what supports a self-service approach. Encouraging clients to select and use these systems offsets the transactional and administrative work that, while integral to HR functions, limits the time available for strategic work.

- *Human Performance Technology (HPT)*. Viewing the organization in both a systemic and holistic manner is a requirement
  when working as an SBP. You will be continually identifying
  the interrelationships between business requirements, the
  performance needs of people, and the work environment of
  the organization. When involved in a performance improvement project, HPT supports the type of analysis you
  will do as you define what performance should be, what it is,
  and what are the root causes for the gap.

- *Organization Development (OD)*. As an SBP, you need to understand how to systemically change an entire enterprise,
  not just a single unit within it. OD provides the knowledge
  of how to define and align the many elements of an organization—its mission, goals, systems, structures, and
  core competence.

The next question is *how* to develop this HR knowledge.
Certainly obtaining degrees in Human Resources from an ac-
credited college or university is one option; in many instances,
having earned a bachelor's or master's degree is a requirement to
moving up the HR career ladder. However, learning must be ongoing and continuous. The field of HR is dynamic and rapidly
changing. New models, systems, technologies, and options are
forming every day. Those with whom we have worked indicate
that they rely on various methods to maintain their knowledge
and stay current in the science of HR. These methods include
joining and participating in professional associations, such as the
Society of Human Resource Management (SHRM), Human
Resource Planning Society (HRPS), and ASTD. We have included a listing of some of these organizations with contact information in the back of this book. Many associations offer
journals that provide articles on HR trends, challenges, and solutions. Certainly, networking with respected colleagues is important, as is reading books published by noted authors and
researchers in the field. And we would be remiss not to mention

the need to seek on-the-job experiences that provide an opportunity to stretch and grow within the HR field. Finally, you will find many books of relevance in the "Resources" section of this book.

Applying Your Business and HR Knowledge

Thus far in this chapter we have focused on what you need to know. Credibility, however, is gained by what you do with what you know. Your on-the-job performance is where the rubber meets the road. Here is a list of practices that successful SBPs use on the job:

- Deliver on commitments made to clients.

- Present proposed plans with a clear financial business case, indicating integration of plan to the current/future requirements of the business. (See the "SBP Example" in this chapter.)

- Connect the dots within and across business units. Talk about initiatives occurring in another part of the business and raise questions about the implications of those initiatives for the business you are supporting.

- In business meetings, offer suggestions and input that goes beyond a strictly HR perspective.

- Verbally and behaviorally demonstrate the belief that you share accountability for business and performance results—not just for the quality of the solutions.

- Be objective in discussions with clients; present your point of view factually and by acknowledging the multiple points of view upon which your perspective is based.

- Push back when the client's preferred action is inappropriate. Indicate your concern when the client's desired results, and the solutions the client is willing to support, are not aligned.

- Underpromise and overdeliver.

- Bring projects in on time and under budget.

Of course, this list has only a few of the many actions you can take to gain credibility with your clients. What is key is to make the development of credibility a goal, taking actions that your clients will value in this regard.

SBP Example

Providing the Business Case for HR Solutions

The Senior VP of Human Resources in a for-profit organization provides an excellent example of working with internal clients as an SBP versus an HR expert. We provide this example here in his words:

"Let's say that my sales organization has lost 40 sales representatives through attrition and career movements. An HR approach to initiating action would be to go to the President with a plan for recruiting 40 sales representatives, replacing those who have left. If I did that, my President would throw me out of his office. As an SBP, I work differently. I obtain the necessary business data and present a business case for the actions needed. This includes identifying the average sales volume being lost per representative, a forecast of the sales environment for the next year, the cost to hire and develop replacements, and the potential payback to the organization over a specific period of time. Using this data, I can present a case for the specific number of sales representatives required, which might not be the same as the 40 representatives who have left. With this approach the President would want to talk."

Something You Can Do

Take a few minutes to identify areas of business and/or HR knowledge you would like to deepen as well as actions you will take to grow this knowledge.

Business Knowledge

If you work internally, consider the organization you are supporting. If you are an external consultant, identify one of the organizations with which you want to form a strong business relationship. Then:

1. Refer to Table 4.1, which describes the business knowledge you need to have about the organization you support and the industry in which it operates. Identify those items for which your knowledge is deep and about which you are confident.

   •

   •

   •

2. Using the same list, identify items where you need to enhance your knowledge relative to the organization you support.

   •

   •

   •

3. Identify the actions you will take to grow your knowledge of the items listed in response to item 2. Use the previous pages in this chapter as a starter list of ideas for actions you might take.

   •

   •

   •

HR Knowledge

1. Listed below are the segments of HR knowledge that were described in this chapter. For each of these, identify whether it is a *strength* or is *needing development.*

Strength		Additional Development Needed
_____	Working Knowledge of Multiple HR Solutions (e.g., recruitment, compensation, training)	_____
_____	Change Management Skill	_____
_____	Formation and Use of a Consulting Model	_____
_____	Knowledge of eHR Systems	_____
_____	Human Performance Technology (HPT) Skill	_____
_____	Organization Development (OD) Knowledge	_____

2. For each area where you have indicated that development is needed, determine one or more actions you can take to increase your knowledge. Consider the actions discussed previously; also review the books in the "Resources" section to identify any that could be helpful to you.

Developing Trust

Building credibility is dependent upon your HR and business capability to deliver results. Trust focuses on how you achieve those

results. Do you accept accountability for both good and poor results? Do you operate in an ethical and authentic manner?

Let's consider a common scenario. Have you ever retained
the services of a consultant who, in your opinion, seemed more
intent on obtaining a contract than on doing what would be most
helpful to you and your organization? Clearly, the consultant had
competence and a great track record that caused you to retain the
consultant in the first place. What you doubted was the *motivation*
by which the consultant operated. Was the motivation to provide
services to benefit your organization *or* was it to sell services in
order to build a larger contract and fee? Your uncertainty about
the consultant's motivation most likely resulted in a lack of trust.

You will know you are trusted when clients seek out your
advice. Other indicators of trust occur when clients share
confidential information or ask you to be present at key
meetings. When a client shares personal anxieties or concerns, you have earned trust at a very high level. One SBP
told us of a client who was leading a major initiative within
the organization. To those on the team, the client evidenced
strong resolve and conviction that the project would be successful despite some significant challenges. But privately to
the SBP, the client expressed deep concerns about the project's success, indicating, "I'm scared to death that this will
not be successful despite all of our efforts." Certainly that
SBP was a trusted confidant.

There are many ways you can build trust with your
clients. One of the most obvious is to maintain confidences
when they are shared. Divulging confidential information
with others is a sure way to kill trust. Another is to honor
commitments you make to clients. Other actions that you can
take to build trust are:

- Ensure that your words and actions are congruent; avoid
  providing mixed messages.

- Act in ways that support the values of your organization.

- When having difficulty with a client, go directly to that in-dividual to discuss the situation. In essence, be a "straight shooter," discussing issues with that person rather than with others *about* the person.

- Be a sounding board on sensitive issues; demonstrate strong listening capability.

- Share your own opinions and perspectives, even when they are different from the majority view. Avoid being a "yes" person.

- Keep your focus on the big picture and the shared goals; help elevate discussions to this level.

- Accept accountability for your own actions and the results of those actions.

- Avoid blaming others; instead focus on what can be done to fix the situation.

These are but a few of many actions that you can take to develop trust. Hopefully, the list provides ideas as to actions you can take to grow trust with your clients.

SBP Tips

1. Credibility is earned over time and leads to client confidence in your capability to deliver results in support of the business. Credibility requires that you have strong knowledge of both HR systems and the "business of the business."

2. Trust is also earned and means that clients have confi-dence in your integrity and reliability to achieve results in support of the business.

3. Each of these requires that you focus on achieving *results*, not just provide *solutions*.

4. Client relationships, including credibility and trust, are developed with people, not with jobs. When the person with whom you have a strong partnership leaves the position and someone new enters the position, the work to build a partnership will begin anew. And relationships are dynamic, not static. Therefore, the A-C-T approach to client relationships will be an ongoing part of your role as an SBP.

PART THREE

IDENTIFYING AND PARTNERING ON STRATEGIC PROJECTS

Figure P3.1 Strategic Business Partner Accountabilities

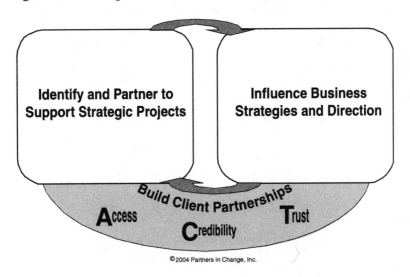

©2004 Partners in Change, Inc.

Once your relationships with clients are at least in the forming stage, it is time to dust off your performance-consulting skills and seek strategic opportunities to work on. We are specifically referring to projects and initiatives within your organization that are integral to business success and have implications for performance of employees and managers. Successful partnering with clients on strategic projects will deepen the credibility and trust with which you are viewed, resulting in greater access and more opportunities. Developing strategic partnerships is truly an iterative process!

There are two ways you can learn of strategic opportunities: reactive and proactive. Each of these approaches requires use of questions that support the logic path described in Chapter 5. In Chapter 6 we explain the reactive approach of reframing a client's request in order to identify strategic opportunities. In the proactive approach, discussed in Chapter 7, SBPs take the initiative to identify strategic opportunities. Regardless of the entry approach, once a strategic opportunity is identified, the next step is to implement the strategic project. Implementation generally requires some level of assessment followed by selection, implementation, and measurement of the necessary solutions. Chapter 8 provides an overview of techniques that SBPs use to accomplish these phases of project work.

Chapter 5

The Logic Used to Identify Strategic Opportunities

"We influence more by what we ask than by what we tell."

Jim and Dana Robinson

You are developing strong partnerships with clients using the A-C-T approach. If these partnerships are similar to those of other Strategic Business Partners (SBPs), some relationships will be deeper and stronger than others. Relationships are dynamic, grow at varying paces, and depend upon the personalities and needs of the people involved. One way to deepen relationships is to effectively deliver on projects and initiatives that support a client's business needs. But first these projects need to be identified.

Often a request from a client provides an opportunity to uncover strategic work. Can you relate to any of these requests?

- "I have two teams who are in continual conflict. I would like to offer some type of team building."

- "I need to redesign my function. Could you assist me in thinking through a new organizational structure?"

- "What training program will enhance the negotiation skills of people in our purchasing group?"

All of these requests are presented in *solution* language; in other words, the clients have identified the specific action they would like to see implemented and are calling you to provide it. We compare these requests to an iceberg. We are learning about the part that is above the water line, while little is known about what lies underneath. By probing to identify both the real need and the desired results, we may uncover a strategic initiative on which to partner. In this way each client request for a solution becomes a situation to be explored. This is what is meant by identifying strategic opportunities in a reactive manner.

A second means of identifying strategic opportunities is to do so proactively. This does *not* mean advocating a solution or action that the client needs to take. Rather you discuss the client's business needs and challenges, potentially discovering a need that, but for this discussion, would not have been known this early.

Each of these approaches requires two skills:

1. Asking thought provoking questions.
2. Using a compelling logic path when asking these questions.

In this chapter we provide techniques regarding each of these skills. These techniques can then be applied whether identifying strategic opportunities reactively or proactively.

Asking the "Right" Questions "Right"

Conversations designed to identify strategic opportunities depend upon your ability to ask the right questions in the most effective manner. These are actually two related, but different, skills. In Chapter 1 we spoke of the use of SHOULD-IS-CAUSE questions; these are the "right" questions. But it is not enough to merely ask a series of questions. It is important to ask them in the "right" manner, using a logic path to guide the process. When you are skillful in this process, you create insights and "a-ha" moments within your client's thinking. The conversation expands the thinking of both of you, yielding a robust amount of information. At minimum you will gain greater clarity on the solution to be implemented; at maximum you will uncover a strategic need to be worked on jointly with the client. You will then have an opportunity to partner with the client to provide results that benefit the business.

The "Right" Questions

As a consultant, it is *not* your responsibility to have the answers. Rather your role is to ask the right questions and partner with clients to determine the answers. Through this partnership you share ownership for results with your client— the only way that sustained results are possible. With so much riding on your questioning skill, let's explore what makes for good questioning.

Consider the questions that appear in Table 5.1. As you review the questions in each column, determine what is different about the questions in Column 1 as compared to the questions in Column 2.

Table 5.1
Two Types of Questions

Column 1	Column 2
• What are the most common errors operators are making now?	• When does the new compensation system need to be implemented?
• In your mind, select the individual who is your best salesperson. What does that person do when closing a call that is successful?	• What is going on?
	• Do people have the skills to do the work?
• What should your turnover rate be?	

The questions on the left are the types of questions you need to ask; these questions have three important characteristics:

1. Open, in that they cannot be answered with a "yes" or "no" response; they require a more complete answer.

2. Focused, in that each question focuses on a specific aspect of the business need (turnover rate) or performance need (closing calls).

3. Bias-free of cause or solution, in that the question does not point to a particular barrier or solution. The question is *solution-neutral.*

The questions in the right column violate one or more of these three principles.

"When does the new compensation system need to be implemented?" is a question that contains an implied solution. It assumes that there will be a new compensation system, and the need is to finalize the time frame for its implementation. "What's going on?" is too broad a question; it is not focused on any specific need or goal. The client could respond with almost any answer, including something that is only marginally relevant to the need being discussed. "Do people have the skills to do this work?" is a question that is both close-ended (can be answered with a "yes" or "no" response) and biased to a cause (lack of skill).

The second required skill is use of a compelling logic path when asking questions. This logic path calls for the three categories of questions, specifically SHOULD, IS, and CAUSE questions. It is important that questions in all three categories be open, focused, and bias-free. Let's look at each category of question in greater detail.

SHOULD *Questions*

Questions designed to determine the desired state either for the business or for the performance of people are called SHOULD questions. When inquiring about business SHOULDs, you are seeking the organization's numerical goals or standards. When focusing on performance SHOULDs, you want to determine the on-the-job practices required for the business SHOULDs focused upon. It is certainly appropriate to ask clients for their opinions as to what people should be doing. (What should people do when they respond to a customer complaint?) Although the client's perspective is important, it is an opinion that may or may not be an accurate or complete description of required practices. So to validate and enhance your client's opinion, you also want to ask star performers about SHOULD performance.

Star performers are individuals who are achieving the business results or are demonstrating the type of performance your client deems worthy. A technique to use is to ask your clients to describe what they see the star performers in their area doing differently from others. (Think of your best Customer Service Representatives (CSRs). What are those CSRs doing differently from others to resolve customer complaints so successfully?) Although clients can typically identify those who are star performers, clients often do not know what these individuals are doing differently to obtain success. This becomes one of those "a-ha" moments, when clients realize that moving to a solution may be premature. They now want to obtain more information to ensure that the solutions utilized will yield desired results.

Once a client acknowledges it is important to obtain performance SHOULD information from star performers, you are in a position to interview, and even observe, these individuals. Star performers can provide a wealth of information as to what they are now doing, as well as what they would *like* to be doing, to accomplish results. Interview just a few star performers and you will have robust behavioral information to share with your client.

IS *Questions*

Just as there are two types of SHOULD questions for business and for performance, there are two types of IS questions. You want to know not only what the desired goals are for the business, but also the actual results at this time. Knowing both SHOULD and IS business information helps you identify the gap in business results. You also want to know what people are *typically* doing compared to what they should be doing; this information will help you identify the performance gaps. You can link SHOULD and IS questions. It is quite natural to ask a client for the production goals followed by a question about the current production rate. You can use this same technique when discussing people's performance. (What do the star performers do to manage projects on time and within budget? And how does that compare to what typical project managers are doing?) Again, the client may be uncertain or may provide only broad descriptions. This creates another opportunity to agree that more information is needed before moving ahead.

CAUSE *Questions*

In Chapter 1 we introduced you to The Gap Zapper; it is illustrated again as Figure 5.1.

Figure 5.1 The Gap Zapper

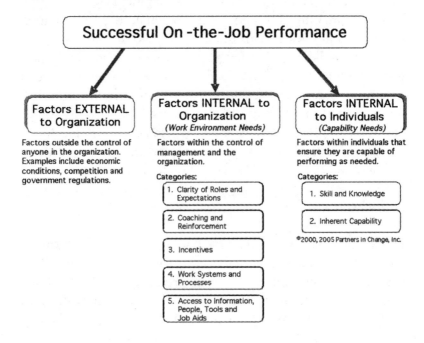

The Gap Zapper identifies the majority of reasons why people do or do not perform as needed. You ask CAUSE questions to identify the reasons or root causes for performance gaps. Essentially CAUSE questions help you to determine which, if any, of the factors within The Gap Zapper are impacting upon people's performance—either by enabling or obstructing it. If you identify factors that enable performance, you want to ensure that those factors are maintained. However, factors that are barriers to performance must be acted upon to diminish their impact or remove them altogether. Because effective performance is usually the result of multiple factors—not a single factor—you want to probe this area in some depth.

Once again, you need to ask open and unbiased questions that focus on both the business and performance areas. A CAUSE question you might ask relative to the business results could be, "What are the primary reasons why our revenue is below plan?" or "Why are the customer satisfaction ratings below goal?" With regards to human performance you could ask, "Why are sales representatives not closing sales?" or "Why are CSRs not effectively managing customer problems and complaints?" CAUSE questions, more than any other question type, help to widen the client's perspective so the situation is viewed in a more systemic, holistic manner.

Something You Can Do

Test your discrimination skills regarding the three types of questions. Below are five questions. Each question is an example of one of the following:

- SHOULD *question*—focuses on obtaining information about the desired business and/or performance requirements.

- IS *question*—focuses on obtaining information about the current business and/or performance results.

- CAUSE *question*—has a purpose of identifying factors that make achieving the desired business and performance results difficult.

- *Biased to a solution/cause question*—an implied solution or cause is embedded in the question. This type of question is to be avoided in initial discussions with clients.

Determine the type of each question. Place a check (✓) in the appropriate box to the right of each question. Use the following key:

S = SHOULD question

I = IS question

C = CAUSE question

B = Biased to a solution/cause question

For each question you indicate as biased in some manner, rewrite the question so it is open, focused, and solution-neutral. Our answers appear at the end of this chapter. We have also included our rationale for our answers.

1. What are you wanting people to do more effectively following the training program?

S	I	C	B

Rewrite of question if "B" is selected: _____

_____

2. You indicated that your team is not getting along. What is happening that leads you to this conclusion?

S	I	C	B

Rewrite of question if "B" is selected: _____

_____

3. What are the primary reasons why our cost of production is higher than the competition?

S	I	C	B

Rewrite of question if "B" is selected: _____

---

4. You mentioned that Sally is very good at building relationships with customers. What does she specifically do that contributes to this result?

S	I	C	B

Rewrite of question if "B" is selected: _____

---

5. Are people being coached and reinforced to perform as needed?

S	I	C	B

Rewrite of question if "B" is selected: _____

Using a Compelling Logic Path

As previously noted, there are two key skills that result in a successful reframing discussion. The first skill is to ask questions that expand the thinking of the client. The second is to ask these questions using a logic path that is helpful and valued by the client. A solid logic path increases the client's confidence that the questioning process will be beneficial and assist in identifying the right solutions. The logic path that has worked for us is illustrated in Figure 5.2 and referred to as a GAPS! Map.

In our book *Performance Consulting* we introduced a tool called the Performance Relationship Map. Over the years we have modified this map and now refer to it as the GAPS! Map.

Figure 5.2 The GAPS! Map

Business Need: _____   Employee Group: _____

(An operational goal for an entity measured   (A specific group of people who
in numbers. The need is typically written in   share the same job or role.)
a narrative manner.)

G

Go
for
the
SHOULD

Business SHOULDs	Performance SHOULDs
List the operational metrics used to measure the business goals. Each metric should have a number.	List the specific, on-the-job behaviors that people in the employee group use to obtain the Business SHOULDs specific behaviors and not vague fuzzy descriptions.

A

Analyze
the
IS

Business IS	Performance IS
List the actual operational results have a number. There should be one IS result for each SHOULD goal noted above	List the actual on-the-job behaviors and practices that people are typically using now. Have at least one actual behavior for each SHOULD behavior noted above. But do not be limited to this list—people could be demonstratlng other behavlors that are using time but providing limited value.

P

Pin
Down
the
CAUSES

Factors External to Organization	Factors Internal to Organization (Work Environment Needs)		Factors Internal to Individuals (Capability Needs)
	Outside the Business Unit	Within the Business Unit	
Identify factors outside the control of anyone in the organization that directly impact upon the business results.	Identify factors within the control of the organization but outside the control of the client(s) accountable for the business results and employee group(s) focused upon.	Identify factors within the control of the organization and within the control of the clients(s) accountable for the business results and employee group(s) focused upon.	Identify skill, knowledge and inherent capability needs of people in the performer group focused upon.

S

Select
the **Right**
SOLUTIONS
© 2002, 2005 Partners in Change, Inc.

Although the format of the map has been modified, the purposes of the map are unchanged:

- Provide a structure into which you can organize information.

- Clearly identify what information is known but also what information, relevant to the situation, is unknown.

- Provide the logic path to use when asking questions of clients.

One of your primary roles as an SBP is to partner with clients to reduce and remove business and performance gaps. We have created the acronym GAPS to assist in remembering the problem-solving process used by SBPs. This acronym indicates both *what* must be obtained and the *order* in which this information is identified.

G = *Go* for the SHOULD. (First identify what is required by the business and from employees.)

A = *Analyze* the IS. (Compare current business results and employee performance to identify the gaps.)

P = *Pin down* the CAUSESs. (Uncover reasons for the gap, ensuring they are root causes and not merely symptoms.)

S = *Select* the SOLUTIONs. (Choose solutions to address root causes, closing the business and performance gaps.)

Employee Groups

Figure 5.2 provides a description of the type of information required for each box. A term in the map that we have not yet discussed is *employee group*. This references the group of people who share a common role or job and who, through their day-to-day performance, most contribute to the business results. Examples are account representatives, project managers, team leads, and production line operators. Employee groups are not departments or functions. For example, the Finance Department is not an employee group; rather, it is a composite of several employee groups. As an SBP you need to identify the specific employee group or groups who are relevant to a situation. If the business goal is broad, there could be more than one employee group that contributes to that business goal. If the business goal in a manufacturing plant is to increase production output, then the employee groups could be the production line operators and their team leads. As an SBP, you unbundle these groups to focus on each separately—creating a GAPS! Map for each unique employee group. Why is this necessary? Because while the business SHOULD and IS information may be identical, the on-the-job performance required of each unique employee group will be different. What operators must do to increase production output will surely be different from what the team leads must do. Also the CAUSE information will be different for each employee group. Highly effective SBPs know that the magic to clarifying a strategic opportunity is to expand the client's thinking while focusing on specifics for the business and the employee groups.

One other item to note about the GAPS! Map is located in the CAUSE section. You will note that the "factors internal to the organization" are divided into two categories—those outside the business unit and those within the business unit. This is important because it separates factors that are outside the client's control from those within the client's control. Factors within the client's control are candidates for solutions that are relatively easy to implement—what some people refer to as low-hanging fruit. Like the apples on a tree that hang low, these solutions are within easy reach. Factors that are outside the client's control, but still within the organization itself, are more challenging to change. This is because clients must influence others to take the needed actions; clients alone cannot authorize the actions because other managers outside the business unit are involved. Therefore, these actions generally require more time to put into effect.

An Example of a GAPS! Map

Figure 5.3 provides an example of a GAPS! Map that has been completed. It supports a project we worked on some years ago in

Figure 5.3 GAPS! Map for a Call Center

Business Need: Employee Group:
Improve Customer Satisfaction Customer Service Representatives (CSRs)

Business SHOULDs	Performance SHOULDs
• 90% of customers are "satisfied" or "very satisfied" with quality of service they receive • 100% of customers' calls picked up within 5 rings • A customer must call only once for a problem to be resolved	• Ask open and focused questions to clarify the customer's problem • Assume "ownership" for resolving the customer's problem • Demonstrate empathy as appropriate • Follow up with customers to provide actions being taken to resolve the problem

G *Go for the* **SHOULD**

Business IS	Performance IS
• 81% of customers are "satisfied" or "very satisfied"; trend line is evidencing a decline in ratings • 88% of customers' calls picked up within 5 rings • Number of customer calls for each problem resolved is 1.4	• Ask closed-ended questions too quickly, narrowing the focus of discussion prematurely • Jump to solutions before problem is completely identified • Rarely assume "ownership" for the problem; tend to transfer customer to another department and disconnect before customer is speaking with the appropriate person • Empathy shown sporadically • Follow-up with customers is inconsistent • Defensive too frequently when the customer is angry

A *Analyze the* **IS**

P *Pin Down the* **CAUSES**

Factors External to Organization	Factors Internal to Organization (Work Environment Needs)		Factors Internal to Individuals (Capability Needs)
• Customer expectations for service continue to increase, raising the standard by which CSR performance is judged	**Outside the Business Unit** • The database used by CSRs is not easily accessible requiring moves between multiple screens to obtain appropriate informaion	**Within the Business Unit** • Insufficient authority to resolve problems independently; CSRs must seek permission to act • Unclear expectations as to what "ownership" means and what actions the CSR should be taking to evidence this accountability • Insufficient coaching and reinforcement from Team Leads	• CSRs lack skill in: ✓Asking open and focused questions ✓Managing customers who are angry

a call center. The business need for this center was to increase customer satisfaction, particularly as it related to how the center responded to problems and complaints of customers. The employee group was comprised of the Customer Service Representatives (CSRs) who worked in the call center.

The GAPS! Map for the call center gives us a picture of the CSRs' goals, performance, and factors that impact their performance and results. Let's look at this picture and draw some conclusions about the CSRs. When we compare the SHOULD information with the IS information, we see gaps in both the business and performance areas. The actual business results are less than the stated goals. At the same time, actual CSR performance differs from the CSR SHOULD performance. Our need is to close gaps in performance and business results. Let's next look at the CAUSE information to determine what factors are impacting CSR performance. The factors internal to individuals indicate that the CSRs lack skill in asking questions and managing angry customers. Clearly, skill development is required. But skill development or training by itself will be insufficient to close the performance gaps. When we look at factors internal to the organization, we see three factors within the business unit that also are causes of the gap. Information about these factors help us to identify appropriate solutions. For example, a solution to extend the authority limits of CSRs to resolve a customer's problem independently would remove one barrier. Clarifying the actions CSRs can take to demonstrate "ownership" of the customer's problem will help to remove another barrier. These solutions are within the client's control and constitute "low-hanging fruit." The problem that the CSRs are having with the database involves the organization's Information Systems Department. Because the client does not directly control the database, he or she will need to involve Information Systems managers to solve the problem. This requires an influencing, rather than a directing, approach. As an SBP, you can coach your client on the most effective approach for discussing the situation with Information Systems. This is an opportunity for you to demonstrate the value that you bring to solving performance problems.

GAPS! Map with Questions

Over the years we have been asked numerous times for a list of questions to use when discussing needs with a client. Unfortunately, there is not a single list of questions that can be used in these discussions. Questions are dependent upon the industry, organization, client, and need. However, in Figure 5.4 we provide a GAPS! Map into which we have placed generic questions. Hopefully this can serve as a thought starter for you in preparing for a conversation with one of your clients.

SBP Tips

1. One of the most significant ways that you add value as an SBP is to identify and support strategic opportunities and projects of importance to your clients. These projects are not just handed to you. Rather, you must be skillful at identifying them. Whether these projects are identified reactively or proactively, you need to use two key skills: asking the "right" questions and using a compelling logic path.

2. The "right" questions are open, focused, and solution-neutral in that they are not biased toward any specific cause or solution.

3. The GAPS! acronym describes the logic path to use:

- *Go* for the SHOULD
- *Analyze* the IS
- *Pin* down the CAUSES
- *Select* the right SOLUTIONS

Figure 5.4 GAPS! Map with Questions

	Business Need: What is the business need?	Employee Group: What work group(s) directly contribute to the achievement of this goal?
G	(An operational goal for an entity measured in numbers.)	(A specific group of people who share the same job or role.)

	Business SHOULDs	Performance SHOULDs
Go **for** **the** **SHOULD**	• What are the goals, objectives or standards? • What are the metrics that need to be achieved? • Is there any business unit/department meet goals? What are their actual results?	• If the goals are to be achieved, what on-the-job performance is required of (*name of work group*)? • If there are star performers, what do they do more, better or differently to achieve these goals?

	Business IS	Performance IS
A *Analyze* **the** **IS**	• What are the actual results? • What are the actual results of typical regions/departments/ groups?	• What do the individuals in the work group typically do? • What have you observed that leads you to believe people will benefit from (*the solution that has been mentioned*)?

	Factors External to Organization	Factors Internal to Organization *(Work Environment Needs)*	Factors Internal to Individuals *(Capability Needs)*
P *Pin* *Down* **the** **CAUSES**	• What are the reasons for the gap between your goals and your actual results? (*Question can yield internal and/or external factors.*)	Outside the Business Unit / Within the Business Unit • What are the reasons for the gap between what people in the work group should be doing and what they are doing? • If the (*solution suggested*) were implemented, what other reasons might still make it difficult for people to perform as needed? • If people in the work group were to develop the skills and knowledge needed, what are the other reasons why they still might not perform as desired?	• How do the capabilities of the work group compare to the requirements of the job?

S *Select* **the Right** **SOLUTIONS**	*Do not ask questions regarding the design and/or implementation of the proposed solution.*

4. The GAPS! Map brings this all together. This map is a tool you use to organize information by identifying the information that is known and relevant to a business and/or performance problem. The GAPS! Map also helps you to determine what is relevant, but unknown about a situation. To adapt an oft-used phrase, you should never leave home without your GAPS! Map!

Answers to Something You Can Do

Now you can compare your answers to ours. We have provided our rationale for the answer that we selected for each question. In some cases you may have selected an answer different from ours. Hopefully, our rationale will help you understand how we viewed the question.

1. Question: What are you wanting people to do more effectively following the training program? Our Answer: BIASED TO SOLUTION **question.** Although this sounds like a SHOULD question, it is really biased to the solution of training. The question asks about SHOULD performance (do more effectively), but it asks for that information on the assumption that people will attend a training program. If the question were, "What is it that you want people to do more effectively?" it would be a SHOULD question that is open, focused, and bias-free.

2. Question: You indicated that your team is not getting along. What is happening that leads you to this conclusion? Our Answer: IS **question.** The question first references a previous statement by the client (your team is not getting along). Then the question asks, "What is happening that leads you to this conclusion?" The question is asking the client to describe his observations of the team and their current on-the-job performance.

3. Question: What are the primary reasons why our cost-of-production is higher than the competition? Our Answer: **CAUSE question.** The question is seeking the primary reasons (causes) for the gap between "our" high cost of production and the competition's lower cost of production. This is an open question that focuses on the causes of a business problem. It is also bias-free of any solution or cause.

4. Question: You mentioned that Sally is very good at building relationships with customers. What does she specifically do that contributes to this result? Our Answer: **SHOULD question.** The question refers to the client's view that Sally is a star performer in that she is "very good at building relationships with customers." Then the question asks, "What does she specifically do?" Because the question asks about the current performance of a star performer, the question yields information about *SHOULD* performance for all people in that work group.

5. Question: Are people being coached and reinforced to perform as needed? Our Answer: **BIASED TO CAUSE question.** This is a binary question (can be responded to in a "yes" or "no" manner) and is focused specifically on one cause (coach and reinforce). A question asked in this manner can put a client on the defensive, because it implies that people are not being coached and reinforced as needed. A better alternative would be to ask, "What makes it difficult for people to perform as you need them to?" Later in the discussion, if you want to know more about a specific factor in The Gap Zapper you might say, "Tell me more about how people are coached and reinforced to perform as you need them to."

Chapter 6

Reframe Requests to Identify Strategic Opportunities

"A prudent question is one-half of wisdom."

Francis Bacon

How often in a month are you contacted by a client who has a request? These requests probably occur with some frequency. Most likely, many of these requests are presented as a Human Resources (HR), Learning, or Organizational Development (OD) solution to be implemented. One option you have is to respond in a tactical manner. With this option you learn more about the employee group and the client's requirements for the solution. Typically, you move quickly toward an agreement to implement the solution. When you use this approach, a request that is presented as a tactical solution remains as such, with the strong probability that it will have modest results. This is because single solutions, by themselves, rarely change performance. Another option is to reframe the request, determining whether there is a strategic opportunity embedded within it. That is the approach we will explore in this chapter.

Reframing—What Is It?

The purpose of reframing is to view a problem or issue from a different point of view. You do this when you facilitate a discussion that focuses *not* on the client's solution but rather on the results the client is seeking. Let us revisit one of the initial requests we used in Chapter 5 as an example.

> "I have two teams who are in continual conflict.
> I would like to offer some type of team building."

Although this client has identified a team-building solution, the client is most likely seeking results that go beyond the team-building activity. Resolving team conflict is probably an ultimate goal, and there could be others. In a reframing discussion you focus not on the solution (team-building activity) but on the desired results (resolving team conflict). Through skillful questioning you help the client gain insight into the situation and to realize that moving ahead with a solution may be premature. Your questions often raise other issues that lead to an agreement to obtain additional information.

In Chapter 1 we introduced you to the Need Hierarchy. This hierarchy indicates the interrelationship of business, performance, work environment, and capability needs. Your goal as a Strategic Business Partner (SBP) is to help clients define and align these needs. The client's request often brings you into the center box of the Need Hierarchy. This is the case when the client requests a work environment and/or a capability solution. As Figure 6.1 illustrates, when you reframe a request, you work from the inner box outward. You acknowledge the need *as presented,* but you do not discuss it at this time. You use the request as an opportunity to discuss performance and business needs that are driving the request.

Figure 6.1 The Direction of Reframing Conversations in the Need Hierarchy

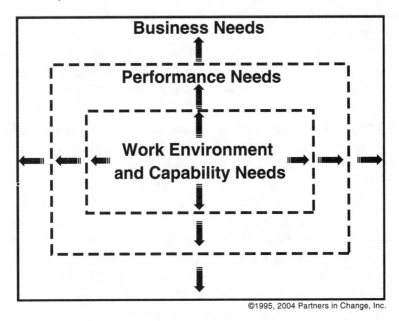

SBP Example

The Power of Asking the "Right" Questions

While at an off-site meeting, Erica reviewed her voice messages. One was from a client who asked that they meet, upon her return, to discuss a need he had to enhance the leadership skills of his supervisors. Erica prepared some SHOULD-IS-CAUSE questions and her logic path for asking these questions; she met with the client shortly after returning to her office.

The need as presented was to provide leadership training—a capability solution request. Erica acknowledged the request and then asked the question, "What have you observed that leads you to believe your supervisors would benefit from leadership training?" This is when Erica learned there was to be a reduction in staff within the client's area, resulting in a loss of approximately eight supervisors. The client wanted the supervisors who remained to be more "empowering" of their employees so that all of the work that remained could be completed. Erica then asked a SHOULD question: "If supervisors were empowering their employees just the way you want them to do, what specifically would they be doing better or differently?" The client indicated that the supervisors would delegate more responsibility to their employees; but beyond that, he was uncertain what it was they should be doing differently. Erica asked, "Is there any supervisor in your team who has demonstrated empowering practices? If so, what is this person doing differently than other supervisors?" The client did acknowledge one individual who was very effective at developing and delegating to his team, but the client was uncertain of the specifics involved. So Erica asked, "Would it be helpful if we worked together to identify the specific practices you need from your supervisory team for them to operate in a way which empowers others?" The client agreed this would be beneficial to do.

Erica did not stop the conversation at this point; she continued to ask some CAUSE questions. One of the questions Erica asked that yielded insight to the client was, "If we were to provide leadership training to your supervisors, so they acquire those skills, what other factors might make it difficult for them to delegate work and empower their employees as you need them to do?" The client acknowledged that the workloads of supervisors were heavy, and that this would only increase when the reduction in staff occurred. He also wondered whether supervisors might be anxious to delegate work to others because the supervisors believe they can do it best. The client acknowledged there could be other factors of which he was not aware. Erica and the client agreed that it would be helpful for Erica to obtain information from the supervisors to determine what are the barriers to empowerment. With this information the client would be in a position to take actions that address root causes and facilitate the performance change needed from supervisors.

The bottom line: Although Erica was asked to deliver a training program, at the conclusion of the meeting the client wanted her help in figuring out what actions were required to take to obtain the performance change he was seeking. Her questioning raised awareness in the client that information needed for success was currently lacking. Without this information the client was jumping to a solution (training) that would require resources of time, money, and people yet yield limited change. Erica helped the client appreciate that both additional information and multiple actions were needed.

Criteria to Qualify a Situation as a "Strategic Opportunity"

The three primary purposes for a reframing meeting are to:

- Determine if the situation qualifies as a strategic opportunity.
- If it qualifies, agree in principle on the information needed before moving forward with solutions.
- If the situation remains as a tactical opportunity, agree on the next steps to be taken towards implementation of that tactic.

We have frequently used the phrase *strategic opportunity*. As noted in Chapter 1, strategic work directly links into one or more business requirements of a business entity and helps move the organization into a favorable position. There are actually five criteria a situation must meet to qualify as a strategic opportunity:

1. There is one or more business needs directly supported by the initiative.

2. The client is seeking performance change from one or more employee groups. The focus is on a group of employees, not on an individual.

3. As the SBP, you will have *direct* access to the client(s) who owns the business need(s) being supported.

4. The client is willing to share accountability with you for producing the required change.

5. The client will provide you with time and access to the appropriate people so you can obtain the required information *before* deciding upon and implementing solutions.

In a reframing discussion, you want to determine which of the preceding criteria are in evidence. To qualify as a strategic opportunity, each criterion must be met or, at minimum, needs to have an absence of a "no." For example, let's assume there is a business need requiring a change in performance of a group of people; therefore, criteria 1 and 2 are affirmed. However, you do not have direct access to the true client because organizational norms require that you work *through* someone else who does have this access. In this instance, criterion 3 is not met. Because it is difficult to influence someone with whom you do not have direct access, the probability of reframing the request into a strategic project is very low. Your role will likely remain tactical for this project.

Another common situation occurs when you learn that there is a business need (criterion 1) and that performance change is required (criterion 2); however, the client has already committed to a specific solution, leaving no time to gain additional information. In this instance you can move the project ahead in a tactical manner, doing what is possible to ensure the solution is implemented well. But there is low probability that the solution will result in long-term, systemic change.

We have also indicated that a criterion may not have a "yes," but it must have an absence of "no" to qualify as a strategic opportunity. The fourth criterion is one that is very difficult to affirm after one meeting with a client. Will this client truly become engaged, taking needed actions? Or will the client become passive, looking to you to do the work? The answers to these questions will occur over some period of time. To view the opportunity as strategic, you need to have reason to think the client *will* be active and share accountability. When uncertain, we assume a "yes" until proven a "no."

Deciding whether to manage the client's need in a strategic or tactical manner is a key benefit resulting from a reframing discussion. It is important to keep in mind that not every situation presented by a client can—or should—be managed strategically. By asking the right questions, you can decide the best way to support the outcomes sought by the client.

Preparing for a Reframing Discussion

Let us assume you have just received a request from a client by e-mail, voice mail, or in a brief face-to-face conversation. Do *not* begin to probe the request immediately unless it is of a transactional nature. Tactical requests require a more in-depth conversation, and one that must be planned. How often will you have an opportunity to discuss and potentially reframe a request with any single client? You want to maximize the probability for success, and this requires planning. We have found that there are three steps in preparing for a reframing discussion.

Step 1. Organize information that is known about the situation into a GAPS! Map.

Step 2. Prepare questions to ask the client about the situation, organizing the questions so they begin with the client's mindset and flow in a logical manner.

Step 3. Prepare the opening statements to be made regarding both the meeting purposes and a summary of known information.

Let's work through these steps with a case example from a company we'll call Cool Age.

Situation Description

Cool Age is a North American-based company that makes air conditioning equipment, compressors, and other temperature control devices for both residential and commercial use. You are an SBP in Cool Age and report into the Corporate Human Resource Department. Your client group is the Marketing and Sales Division. This division is responsible for sales to heating and air conditioning contractors and to retail stores. Customers come to these stores to purchase Cool Age equipment. There are more than 150 people in the Marketing and Sales Division, the majority of whom are Territory Managers. An organization chart for Cool Age and the Marketing and Sales Division appears in Figure 6.2.

You have just received a call from the Vice President (VP) of Marketing and Sales. He is quite concerned and is seeking your help. For the past two years, the profits from this division have been trending downward. One reason for this is the lower pricing offered by competitors for comparable products, a tac-

Figure 6.2 Cool Age and the Marketing and Sales Division

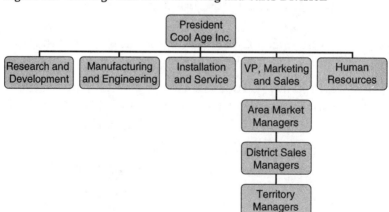

tic being used to gain market share. This puts pricing pressure on Cool Age and is contributing to a reduction in profits.

For the next fiscal year, the priority is to improve corporate profits while continuing to meet revenue goals. Territory Managers (TMs) contribute to profits by negotiating for sales contracts with their retail customers. The TMs have some latitude in how they price Cool Age products to retailers. The Marketing and Sales Department has developed guidelines to provide a range of acceptable discounts. The goal is to negotiate toward the higher end of the range. However, TMs can use discretion based upon other factors such as the volume of business a retailer is doing with Cool Age. The higher the volume, the more the pricing can be discounted.

The VP is convinced that TMs are too quick to sell to the retailer at the lower end of the range. TMs are focused on revenue far more than on profit. TMs are bonused based upon achievement of their revenue goal; there is no bonus focused on the profitability of their sales. In order to ensure that TMs keep their eye on profits as well as on revenue, the VP wants to modify the bonus plan. He has asked to meet with you to discuss the plan's design and implementation.

What an opportunity for a reframing discussion! The person who has called is certainly the owner of the business need to grow profitable revenue. And he certainly knows that a key to success is through the performance of a group—the TMs. The problem? He has jumped to a compensation solution and has called for your help. Although such a plan may be required, it is doubtful that, by itself, a revised bonus plan will achieve the client's profitability goals. Let us look at how to prepare for this reframing discussion.

Step 1: Organize Information That Is Known into a GAPS! Map

First you want to clarify what is known, as well as what is unknown but relevant and important, to achieving the client's goal of profitable revenue. The GAPS! Map is a tool to assist you in this process. The information that is unknown becomes the basis for the questions you will ask in the meeting. By organizing information in this manner, you are also mapping the client's perspective or mindset. It is vital to know what the client thinks and use that perspective as the starting point for your questions. By writing information into the GAPS! Map, you *are not* agreeing that the information is accurate, complete, or valid. Instead you *are* indicating what your client believes to be important regarding the situation. You are mapping the client's mindset.

Something You Can Do

1. Review the Cool Age information described in the Situation Description on the previous pages and place that information in the appropriate areas on the GAPS! Map that appears in Figure 6.3. We have begun the map by indicating both the business need and employee group to be focused upon.

2. When writing information into the map, make no assumptions or inferences. Use only the information as provided. This will help you to remain bias-free of any cause or solution at this early stage in the process.

3. Compare your map to the one that appears at the end of this chapter as Figure 6.8. That map shows how we place the Cool Age information into the GAPS! Map.

Step 2: Prepare Questions to Ask, Organizing Questions So They Begin with the Client's Mindset and Flow in an Organized Manner

What is the probability that changing the bonus plan, as the client has suggested, will be an appropriate solution for this situation? It does seem logical to align the bonus plan for TMs with the corporate profit goals. What is the probability that this one

Figure 6.3 The GAPS! Map

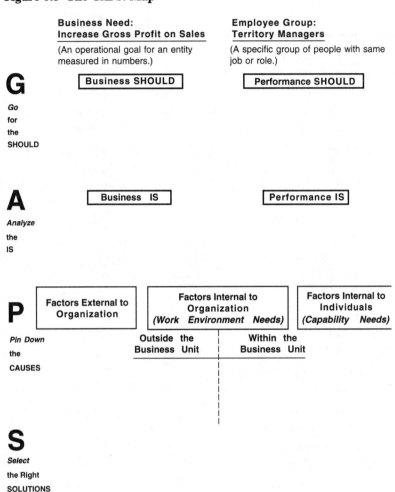

© 2002, 2005 Partners in Change, Inc.

change, by itself, will be sufficient to change the performance of TMs and achieve the profit goals? It is unlikely that this—or any single solution—will be sufficient. But what else is required? Based upon what you know now, you can only guess. So you must make a choice. One option is to operate in a tactical manner. In this approach you identify the requirements for the new bonus plan and set to work designing and implementing it. Another option is to be more objective and unbiased. In this approach you conduct a reframing discussion to determine whether the situation is one that would be best served by a more strategic approach. This is, of course, what we are encouraging you to do!

In preparing for the meeting, you want to develop starter questions to ask the VP once you are having the discussion—a discussion that can occur on the phone or face to face. E-mail is *not* an option. You need an opportunity to probe and build upon comments made by the client in a real-time manner.

Forming the questions to ask is an important task in planning for the meeting. But you also need to organize the questions into the logic path you will use in the meeting. To do this we encourage you to (a) enter the map by asking questions about the highest-level need (in the Need Hierarchy) that the client has provided and (b) ask all remaining questions to explore that need thoroughly before transitioning to the other side of the GAPS! Map. Let us look at an example.

Suppose a client phoned you with this request: "My managers need to persuade others, not directly under their control, to use the project management tools that we have developed. What type of training do you have to increase the influencing skills of these managers?"

Two needs in the hierarchy have been identified: performance need (my managers need to persuade others to use project management tools) and a capability need (what type of training do you have to increase the influencing skills of these managers). If you place these two needs into the Need Hierarchy, as shown in Figure 6.4, it is quickly apparent that the performance need is the higher-level need. Given this, you want to begin asking your questions about that need.

By starting with a performance question, you are acknowledging the client's mindset. You are starting your questions with the highest need stated by your client. You could begin your discussion by asking, "If managers were successfully influencing others regarding these tools, what would those managers be doing?" or "Is there any manager who is successfully influencing others to use these tools? What is that

Figure 6.4 Need Hierarchy

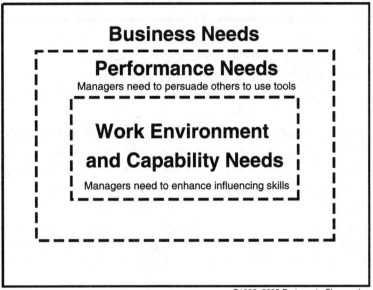

manager doing to effectively influence others?" Answers to either question will provide you with more complete performance SHOULDs. When you have sufficient SHOULD performance information, you can continue by asking performance IS questions. A question you might ask is, "Given this is what you want the managers to be doing, what are you observing these managers do now?" The CAUSE question you might ask is, "Why do you believe the managers are not influencing others as you want them to do?" After exploring the performance need in some depth, you then transition to the business side of the GAPS! Map. An example of how to do this would be to ask, "If managers were successful at influencing others to use these tools, how would this impact the business results for your area?"

What if the only need provided by a client is a solution? For example, suppose a client sent you an e-mail with the following request. "I want to put my team through some type of 360°

feedback experience. Please give me a call so we can discuss this." In this example, you do not want to discuss this solution. Instead, you want to discuss the results the client is seeking from the 360° feedback experience. An effective technique is to acknowledge the request and follow with a question that focuses the discussion on performance issues. You could ask something like this, "You indicate that the team would benefit from some type of 360° feedback experience. What have you observed in their performance that leads you to believe this would be a helpful experience for your team at this time?" This question moves the focus of the discussion from a solution to the performance of the team. After discussing team performance, you can ask about and discuss business results. Discussions about business and performance gaps will highlight areas where your client seeks improvement. This focus on performance and business needs will often lead to the identification of strategic projects.

Something You Can Do

What are the starter questions you want to ask the VP of Marketing and Sales in the Cool Age situation? The questions you ask need to focus on each specific part of the GAPS! Map. You want to come to a reframing meeting with at least one starter question for each part of the GAPS! Map.

1. Review the completed GAPS! Map in Figure 6.8 at the end of this chapter. Start with the business SHOULD box and form one question you want to ask. You can input these questions into the map in Figure 6.5.

2. Now move to the performance SHOULD box. What question might you ask the VP regarding what the TMs need to be doing?

3. Ensure that questions are open, focused to one part of the map, and bias-free of any cause or solution.

You may want to refer to Figure 5.4 in Chapter 5 for some question ideas.

4. Continue through the GAPS! Map, forming one question for each box within the map.

5. When completed, compare your questions to those appearing in Figure 6.9 at the end of this chapter. These are provided as examples and are not intended to be the only options possible.

Figure 6.5 Cool Age GAPS! Map
Questions to Ask VP of Marketing and Sales

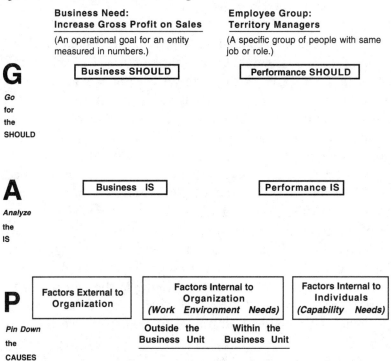

© 2002, 2005 Partners in Change, Inc.

It is important to note that the questions you develop should be viewed as a starter kit and not a complete list of questions. You prepare questions to ensure that the discussion does move to each major portion of the GAPS! Map. However, during the meeting you will learn more information about the situation from the client. You want to use this client information to form additional questions—questions not possible to create in advance.

Finally, in preparing questions you want to identify where to enter the GAPS! Map and how to proceed around the map from that point. This is what we mean by forming a logic path for questioning the client. Keep in mind that the guideline is to begin the questioning process by focusing on the highest-level need as presented by the client. With that in mind, where would you begin the discussion with the VP of Marketing and Sales in Cool Age? Because the VP provided information about a business need (to increase gross profit on sales), you will begin at that level. You want to deep-drill the business side of the map, obtaining as much information as possible. When you have uncovered a gap between SHOULD and IS for the business, ask your CAUSE questions. Once you have obtained sufficient information for the business side of the map, you transition to the performance side and continue the discussion. A good transition statement in this case would be, "Clearly the TMs are key in obtaining the profit goals you have mentioned. What is it that they need to do differently if they are to successfully negotiate pricing at the higher end of our acceptable range?" Figure 6.6 illustrates the logic path to use when beginning a reframing discussion on the business side of the map.

But what if the need as presented by the client includes only a performance need, and not a business need? Then you enter the map on the performance side, obtaining SHOULD, IS, and CAUSE questions regarding the on-the-job performance of people in a specific employee group. Using the Cool Age example again, let's change the presenting need. In this example,

Figure 6.6 Logic Path Used When Beginning on the Business Side of the GAPS! Map

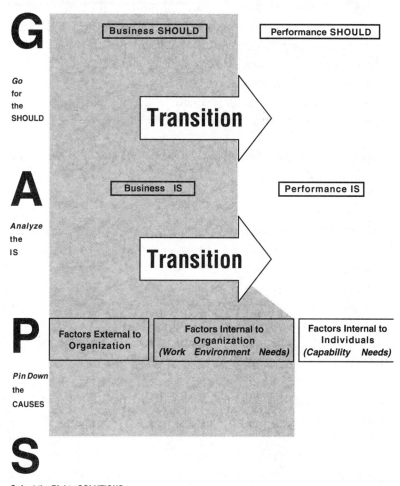

G

Go for the SHOULD

| Business SHOULD | | Performance SHOULD |

Transition

A

Analyze the IS

| Business IS | | Performance IS |

Transition

P

Pin Down the CAUSES

| Factors External to Organization | Factors Internal to Organization *(Work Environment Needs)* | Factors Internal to Individuals *(Capability Needs)* |

S

Select the Right SOLUTIONS

© 2002, 2005 Partners in Change, Inc.

the client has called and indicated that TMs need to do a better job of negotiating sales at the higher end of the profit range. There is no business need identified in the request. In order to connect with the client, we will begin with questions on the performance side of the map. An example would be, "What specifically do TMs need to do differently to negotiate sales at the higher end of the profit range?" You would obtain information regarding what TMs should do, what they are doing, and reasons for the gap. Then you transition to the business side of the map with a statement such as, "If TMs were negotiating more profitable sales with their customers, what operational results would you expect to see?" You continue the discussion to obtain SHOULD, IS, and CAUSE information regarding the business need. Figure 6.7 illustrates the logic path used in this type of situation.

Step 3: Prepare the Opening Statements to Be Made Regarding Meeting Purposes and Summary of Known Information

Now you have prepared your questions, but the conversation will not start with a question. You want to put the meeting into context and transition into the questioning process. You need to identify your purposes for the meeting and seek from the client what he or she would like to accomplish. When forming meeting purposes, keep the focus on the *results* to be achieved, not the *solution* requested. In the Cool Age situation, a solution purpose would be to clarify the requirements for the revised compensation plan. This would be a purpose that focuses directly on the solution. A results-focused purpose would be to gain a greater understanding of the business drivers behind the request as well as to more clearly understand the performance required of TMs if profit goals are to be achieved. You also want to indicate your intent to leave the meeting with clarity on the next steps needed to address the problem. In other words, your purposes are to obtain information *and* to form an action plan. In addition, you want to prepare a brief summary of what you know about the situation. Be clear on how you will begin the meeting, as well as the questions to ask, so that you can manage the time spent with the client as effectively as possible.

Figure 6.7 Logic Path Used When Beginning on the Performance Side of the GAPS! Map

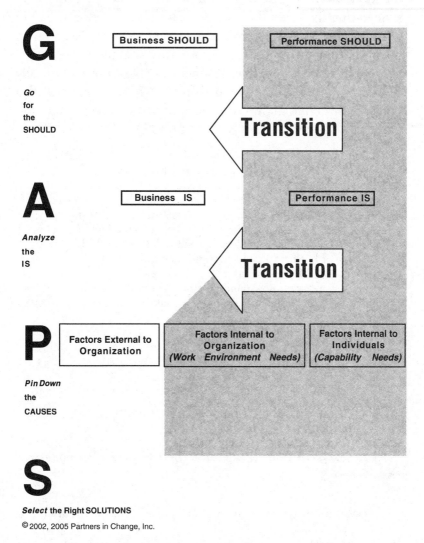

© 2002, 2005 Partners in Change, Inc.

Conducting a Reframing Meeting

Let's now look at how you conduct a reframing meeting. As noted previously, a reframing meeting can be managed in a face-to-face manner or on the phone. A minimum of 30 minutes is required, but 60 minutes is preferred. This meeting is the moment of truth—when you put to use the techniques described thus far. Over the years we have had the opportunity to observe more than 1,000 reframing meetings, providing us with the opportunity to identify the process and techniques that most frequently result in a successful meeting. The process typically utilized is displayed in Table 6.1. In the "Tools" section of this book, you will find an interview format that can be used to prepare for, and conduct, this type of meeting.

Table 6.1
Steps in a Reframing Meeting

---

1. Confirm and agree with the client on the purposes for the meeting.
2. Confirm, in a brief manner, your understanding of the situation.
3. Ask SHOULD-IS-CAUSE questions, beginning with the highest-level need expressed by the client. Explore that side of the GAPS! Map (performance or business) completely and then transition to the other side of the GAPS! Map to ask additional questions.
4. Summarize what is known and unknown about the situation, determining whether the situation should be managed as a *tactical* or *strategic* opportunity.
5. If it is a strategic opportunity, agree on the type of information that must be obtained and form an action plan for obtaining this information. If it is tactical, determine the next steps required to prepare for and implement the solution focused upon.
6. Seek and respond to client concerns and finalize next steps for both you and the client.

Step 1: Confirm and Agree with the Client on Purposes for the Meeting

In this step use the comments you prepared prior to the meeting.

Step 2: Confirm Your Understanding of the Situation

Again, use the comments you prepared prior to the meeting. You typically will spend less than five minutes on Steps 1 and 2. The purpose of these two steps is to provide context to the discussion and to establish the parameters for it. Go through your prepared comments quickly, seeking input from your client as you planned.

Step 3: Ask SHOULD-IS-CAUSE Questions

In this step you ask your prepared questions beginning with the highest-level need expressed by your client. Remember that your prepared questions are starter questions used to begin a discussion in one part of the map. When your client provides some information in response to your question, you form additional questions to deep-drill the information being discussed. You use the deep-drill questions to obtain information needed to determine if the situation should be managed as a tactical or strategic opportunity. These questions will also help identify what is known and unknown about the situation.

Step 4: Summarize What Is Known and Unknown

In this step you first summarize what is known and then follow with any content areas in the GAPS! Map where information is unknown or uncertain. It then becomes relatively easy for your client to see the importance of obtaining this information. Your logic path is one of the most effective skills for selling the client on the value of obtaining more information.

Another element of this fourth step is to decide whether to manage the situation in a strategic or tactical manner. To qualify as a strategic opportunity, the situation needs to meet the five criteria discussed earlier in this chapter. Remember, a strategic situation meets all five criteria or, at minimum, the criteria have the absence of a "no" response. When uncertain, give the situation the benefit of the doubt until proven otherwise. In a strategic opportunity the next step will *always* be to obtain more information. How to obtain that information is discussed in Chapter 8. With a tactical opportunity the next step is to plan the implementation of that solution. It is worth repeating a previous comment: Not every tactical request can, or should, be managed in a strategic manner. It is up to you to make the appropriate judgment given the information learned and the results required.

Step 5: Agree on Next Steps

You want to affirm the steps that will follow from this reframing meeting. When a strategic opportunity has been identified, you often want some time to reflect on how best to obtain the needed information. You also may need to form a project team if the project is large. Tell the client that you need time to develop a plan and will return with a proposal. For a tactical situation you may decide to form the action plan with the client at this time.

Step 6: Seek and Respond to Client Concerns

Now you discuss any concerns or questions the client may have. It is also vital to agree on next steps that you and the client will be taking. Although your next steps could be to develop an action plan, your client may need to obtain some information to help form the plan. Look for ways to meaningfully involve the client right away. There is not much of a partnership if you are the only one with tasks to complete!

SBP Example

Obtaining a "Yes" to Analysis without Using the Word

Dana was consulting with a large petroleum company some years ago. She was partnered with the Director of Learning and Development (L&D); together they met with the Plant Manager of one of the company's larger refineries. This Plant Manager had contacted the L&D Director, indicating that the refinery was experiencing some serious problems with profitability and cost of production. The Plant Manager requested training for the operators to help them become more efficient in the way they work.

In the reframing meeting the discussion began with several questions about the business needs of plant profitability and production costs. Because the Plant Manager had provided these business needs when presenting the request to the L&D Director, it was appropriate to begin the questioning by focusing on those needs. As the meeting progressed, Dana made a transition to the performance side of the GAPS! Map. She asked the Plant Manager, "What groups of employees in the plant will most affect a change in plant profitability through their day-to-day performance?" The Plant Manager responded that the operators were the group to be focused upon. Dana then asked, "What do your operators need to do more, better, or differently if you are to achieve your profitability goals?" The Plant Manager paused, then responded, "I don't know, but that's a mighty fine question!" Dana then asked, "Would it be helpful to have that information?" He responded "You betcha!" Nowhere in the discussion were the terms *analysis* or *assessment* used. Rather, the client was acknowledging the value of obtaining an answer to a question about resolving his business problem. This reframing discussion led to a project where the L&D Director and Dana became SBPs, supporting the Plant Manager in his goal to achieve plant profitability. The focus was on the business results desired and not on any single solution.

Core Behaviors That Need to be Evidenced in Reframing Meetings

The following behaviors are not linked to any specific step in the reframing process; they are to be used as needed during the meeting.

Restate and Summarize What is Said, Connecting the Dots When Possible.

Restating information is a good way to ensure you understand what the client is expressing, but successful SBPs take this further. They summarize by acknowledging some information obtained early in the conversation, linking it to information being discussed at the moment. This is called connecting the dots, with each data point qualifying as one of these dots.

Deep Drill Key Issues

Frequently, clients provide information in vague language. For example, a client might indicate that her team needs to be "more collaborative and supportive of each other." You should turn that information into a question by asking, "What is it that team members do to be more collaborative and supportive?" More than any other technique, the deep-drilling of client responses is likely to uncover uncertainty on the part of the client, resulting in interest to obtain more information.

Cash In on What Is Unknown

This equates to closing the sale. When a client responds with "I don't know" to a question, you ask if it would be helpful to obtain that information. If the client says "yes," you have cashed in—you have closed the sale. Do not let these opportunities pass you by!

Push Back When the Client's Solution Is Inappropriate

When clients identify specific performance and/or business results they seek but then evidence intent to implement a solution that will not provide those results, it is vital that you express your concern. By not expressing concern, you are implicitly endorsing the proposed plan. Then, when the solution is implemented, but the intended results do not occur, you may lose credibility with your client. You have also contributed to a waste of valuable resources. For example, suppose your client has asked for your help in facilitating a team-building session for a group that does not work well together. Through your reframing discussion you have determined that building awareness about effective team work could be helpful, but that this action alone will be insufficient for the changes desired by the client. Perhaps there are structural problems, conflicting roles, unrealistic expectations, or a work process that is causing team conflict. If the client insists on a team-building experience as the *only* solution to be taken, what do you do? You can push back through a question such as, "If we deliver the team-building experience, which we *can* do, what are other reasons why the team members would still not perform as you need them to do?" You can also push back more directly by stating your concern that team building, by itself, will not yield the results the client seeks and giving your reasons for this conclusion. Pushing back does not automatically mean that clients will change their point of view. It does mean that you are working in an authentic manner with your clients and not just as a pair of hands or an order taker.

Be Prepared to Exit Entirely

In Step 4 of a reframing discussion, you make a decision about whether the situation should be managed in a tactical or strategic manner. There is the possibility, however, that the optimal next step is to exit the situation altogether. When might this occur? Perhaps the situation, as you now understand it, would best be managed by a colleague in another group; the need can then transfer to someone else who will benefit from the information you have obtained. Perhaps the client has determined that he or she is not ready to proceed. You have raised sufficient questions in the client's mind to make additional preparation time a valued next step. In this case you exit the situation, at least for now, while your client does the necessary homework. One SBP in a multinational corporation with whom we work indicates that for every ten requests he receives and manages through a reframing process, approximately half never move forward. And this is a decision his clients support! The result is that the resources of the SBP and his team are focused only on those needs where the probability of success is good to excellent. An additional benefit is that his clients are spared the expense of implementing solutions with limited results. And throughout the process, clients are learning that obtaining business and performance results is generally more complex than any single solution can deliver. It is a win for all involved.

SBP Tips

1. As an SBP you want to identify strategic opportunities to partner with your clients. Reframing requests for solutions is one way to do this. Not every request can, or should, be managed in a strategic manner. But every tactical request *should be* reframed and explored for that possibility. Those situations that meet the five criteria given in this chapter are opportunities for strategic work.

2. Reframing is a process for transitioning a client request for a solution into a discussion of business and performance needs. Good planning is key to meeting success. You can plan how to open a reframing meeting and which starter questions to ask. However, much of the success of the meeting results from your deep-drilling of information that the client provides. It is this technique that facilitates client insight regarding the need for additional information.

3. When reframing is done successfully, you will find that a percentage of requests that originate as tactical requests will reframe into more strategic opportunities. And successfully working those projects will continue to enhance your credibility and trust with the client.

4. One benefit from reframing is that a certain percentage of requests made by clients will not proceed beyond the initial meeting, and the client will be endorsing that action. Reframing is a powerful tool you want to use as skillfully as possible.

Answers to *Something You Can Do*

We placed the information regarding the Territory Managers in the GAPS! Map shown in Figure 6.8. Compare your GAPS! Map with this map. This is the only information that is known at this time. Clearly there is much to be discussed with your client.

In figure 6.9 we have developed starter questions for each box within the SHOULD, IS, and CAUSE areas of the GAPS! Map. Compare your questions to ours. Certainly, we do not expect your questions to be identical to ours. However, it is important that your questions:

• Are open, focused on one part of the map, and bias-free of a cause or solution.

• Reflect the information provided about the Cool Age TMs and the business need of increasing gross profit on sales.

Note that there are no questions focused on the solution requested by the VP of Marketing and Sales. If you ask questions about the proposed solution to modify the bonus plan for TMs and how this can be done, you are implicitly endorsing that solution.

Figure 6.8 GAPS! Map with Information as Presented by Retail VP

Business Need: **Increase Gross Profit on Sales**	**Employee Group:** **Territory Managers**
(An operational goal for an entity measured in numbers.)	(A specific group of people with same job or role.)

G

Go
for
the
SHOULD

Business SHOULDs	Performance SHOULDs
• Improve corporate profits • Continue to meet revenue goals	• Negotiate sales to retailers with a goal of agreeing to pricing that is at the higher end of the range • Use judgment when agreeing on price with retailers, considering factors such as volume of business the retailer is doing with Cool Age

A

Analyze
the
IS

Business IS	Performance IS
• Profits trending down	• Too quick to sell retailer at lower end of acceptable range • TMs focus on revenue more than they focus on profit

P

Pin Down
the
CAUSES

Factors External to Cool Age	Factors Internal to Cool Age *(Work Environment Needs)*	Factors Internal to Individuals *(Capability Needs)*
• Competitors charging lower prices for comparable products	Outside the Business Unit (Outside Marketing and Sales Division)	Within the Business Unit (Within Marketing and Sales Division)
		• Pricing guidelines provide a range of acceptable discounts • TMs have some latitude in how they price to retailers • Bonus based on meeting revenue, not profit, goal

S

Select
the Right
SOLUTIONS

© 2002, 2005 Partners in Change, Inc.

Figure 6.9 Cool Age GAPS! Map
Possible Questions to Ask the VP of Marketing and Sales

Business Need: Increase Gross Profit on Sales	Employee Group: Territory Managers

G

Go
for
the
SHOULD

Business SHOULD	Performance SHOULD
What are goals for gross profit on sales? You want to meet revenue goals. What are these goals?	*Are there any TMs who are successful at negotiating sales at the higher end of our range? If yes, what are they doing differently to accomplish this result?*

A

Analyze
the
IS

Business IS	Performance IS
You indicate that profits are trending down. What are the current results?	*Given what the most effective Territory Managers are doing to successfully negotiate sales at the higher end of the range, how does that compare to what the "typical" Territory Manager is doing?*

Factors External to Cool Age	Factors Internal to Cool Age *(Work Environment Needs)*	Factors Internal to Individuals *(Capability Needs)*
	Outside the Business Unit Within the Business Unit	

P

Pin
Down
the
CAUSES

You indicated that our competitors are placing pressure on our pricing of products by selling comparable products at lower prices. Are there any other factors, outside of Cool Age, that challenge the accomplishment of our profit goals?	*What factors, if any, within our organization make it difficult for Territory Managers to negotiate pricing with retailers as you need them to do?* *If we successfully redesign the bonus plan so TMs are compensated in meeting the profit goals, are there any other factors that will still challenge TMs as they work to support these profit goals?*	*What is your assessment of the capability of our Territory Managers to perform as you need them to do?*

S

Select
the Right
SOLUTIONS

Do not ask questions regarding the design and/or implementation of the proposed solution.

Chapter 7

Proactively Identify Strategic Opportunities

> "Proactive\adj. Creating or controlling a situation by taking the initiative."
>
> The Oxford Encyclopedic English Dictionary

As a Strategic Business Partner (SBP), you have developed partnerships with key leaders in your organization. You have developed access to these managers who view you with credibility and trust. But relationships are of little value in themselves; you want to leverage those relationships to identify and partner on strategic projects for which the value to the business is evident. As discussed in Chapter 6, you can identify these types of projects in a reactive manner. But there are obvious challenges involved with this approach—including the fact that once a client contacts you with a request, there may be limited time or interest to reframe the need.

Therefore, it is vital that you seek strategic opportunities in a proactive manner. Although there are many techniques used in a reactive approach that can be used in a proactive discussion, there are also some critical differences. Let's look more deeply into conducting proactive conversations.

What Is a Proactive Conversation?

In Chapter 6 we indicated that conversations begin with the highest-level need in the Need Hierarchy presented by the client. In a reactive discussion the client determines where to begin by presenting a request; typically this includes a solution request that places you into the inner box. Your goal is to transition from the inner box (work environment and capability needs) to the outer boxes (performance and business needs). In a proactive conversation, *you* are initiating the conversation. This provides you with the opportunity to determine where to begin. And, of course, the place you want to begin the discussion is with the business needs. Figure 7.1 illustrates this dynamic of a proactive conversation in which you move from the business needs through performance needs into a discussion of work environment and capability factors.

Figure 7.1 The Direction of Proactive Conversations in the Need Hierarchy

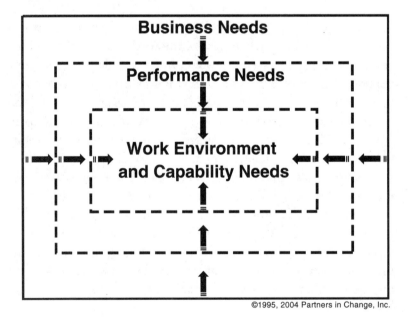

©1995, 2004 Partners in Change, Inc.

A major benefit of a proactive conversation is that projects identified in these conversations are almost always strategic. And when you identify a strategic opportunity in this manner, you are usually entering the project earlier in the decision-making process than is true with projects identified reactively. This means there are more options available as you are engaging with the client when the situation is more fluid. This provides you with more opportunities to influence the decisions being made. And your credibility with clients is enhanced when you are instrumental in proactively identifying a strategic business need on which to partner.

SBP Example

Identifying a Strategic Project Proactively

It was early in the new fiscal year, and Allison had made appointments to meet with her key clients in the Sales and Marketing Department. Each appointment was to be approximately 60 minutes in length. Allison's goals were to discuss the client's business needs for the coming year so she would gain greater insight into the goals and challenges for the department. She also hoped to identify a strategic opportunity on which to partner.

Allison conducted one of her proactive conversations with the Vice President (VP) of Sales. In this discussion he indicated that a key business goal for his area was to double revenue and triple profits within the next three years. He had established milestones for progress towards this goal for the current fiscal year. He acknowledged that these were aggressive goals and provided Allison with both the business drivers for the initiative as well as some strategies that were being implemented to accomplish the goal.

Allison asked the VP, "What groups of employees within the Sales and Marketing Department will most contribute to this revenue and profit goal through their day-to-day performance?" The VP identified three specific jobs, indicating the position of Area Sales Manager (ASM) was of greatest interest. ASMs have large territories and manage account managers who call upon customers for the purposes of selling services and to maintain the relationships with their customers. Each ASM had an aggressive revenue and profit goal to achieve in the current year. Allison asked, "What do ASMs need to do more, better, or differently if they are to achieve these goals?" The VP revealed that he was uncertain and that this was a question that kept him up at night. Then Allison asked, "Would it be helpful if I worked with you and others in the department to answer that question?" The VP indicated that he would find this most helpful.

As a result of this conversation, Allison identified a strategic opportunity to partner in a proactive manner. Working with a project team, she developed a performance model that answered the question of what ASMs had to do differently if they were to successfully support the revenue and profit goals. The performance model also included information about the current work environment, including some factors that would be barriers to ASMs performing as required. The information in the performance model enabled the VP and Allison to develop solutions to improve the sales capability of ASMs while also enhancing their work environment. Allison's proactive discussion with her client uncovered a strategic opportunity that may have otherwise been missed.

Techniques for Identifying Strategic Opportunities Proactively

The first step to working on a strategic project is to obtain one! So how *do* you identify these business-linked projects in a proactive manner? Certainly, a relationship with clients who own these types of needs and requirements is mandatory—a relationship based upon A-C-T. Deep knowledge of the business will also be a requirement. A third key is the capability of connecting what may appear to be disparate pieces of information; it is through the linkage of these data points that you may identify a need. As one SBP said, "It's as if I am at the one thousand-foot level looking down on the various parts of the organization. I try to identify what is missing or what may be heading to a conflict or crisis. Then I meet with the appropriate managers to determine if they have a similar perspective. In the process we may unearth an opportunity on which to partner."

As an SBP, you have an opportunity to leverage this 1,000-foot perspective of the organization when you work on project teams or when you attend client staff meetings. In each instance business information is being shared and business challenges identified. You can look for what is missing or where the potential conflicts or crises may be. By articulating your observations, you may raise awareness of a need. Often the need requires obtaining information to clarify what is currently unknown or vague—an entry point for most strategic work.

Another way in which you can proactively identify strategic opportunities is to stay current with business and industry trends. Reviewing Web sites relevant to your organization, learning what your organization's competitors are doing, keeping abreast of breakthrough thinking and concepts regarding how to optimize the people's performance—all of these are excellent ways to identify strategic opportunities. Many SBPs send articles focusing on a new idea or trend to their sustained clients and follow that with a call to discuss this trend's implications for the client's organization.

One preferred method for staying current with a client's business needs is to schedule a 60- to 90-minute conversation with a sustained client. The purpose of the discussion is to deepen knowledge of your client's business; the purpose is *not* to discuss Human Resource (HR) products and services. We are continually amazed at both what is learned in these discussions as well as the eagerness with which sustained clients participate in them. We recall one situation in which an SBP made an appointment with a director who, when confirming the appointment, requested that they meet in a conference room with a white board. When the time came for the meeting, the director brought in several documents for the SBP and used the white board to illustrate initiatives and items of relevance to his business. The conversation continued past the one hour of time that had been scheduled and resulted in the identification of a project for the SBP to work on. For the most part, managers *want* SBPs to know about and support their business goals. Because this proactive approach is so effective, we want to discuss it in some depth.

Conducting Proactive Conversations

Proactive conversations are generally conducted with sustained clients. Ideally, these conversations occur in a planned manner throughout the fiscal year—perhaps at the start of the year and again on a quarterly or biannual basis. There are two purposes for these conversations:

1. *To deepen your personal knowledge and stay current about the business of your sustained clients.* Although information is always available, it often comes in small nuggets. You learn one piece of information in a meeting and another piece when talking to a manager on the way to your office. The advantage of a proactive conversation is the concentrated amount of time that is dedicated to a systematic look at the business. You can also probe and explore information about the business in depth.

2. *To identify potential strategic opportunities on which to partner.* These are strategic projects that would, in most likelihood,

not have been identified this early except through the proactive conversation. A proactive conversation is a type of marketing vehicle for the SBP because it helps to identify *additional* strategic projects on which to partner.

Our criteria to judge success of a proactive conversation are simple:

- Is the client engaged in the conversation, as was the manager who actively drew on the white board and brought documents for the SBP to review?
- Is the client amenable to continuing this type of dialogue in the future?

If, in fact, a strategic project is identified, all the better; but we do not view this as the primary purpose for the meeting. In the end, you have these types of discussions to enhance and deepen your partnership with your clients.

Preparing for the Conversation

You have scheduled a one-hour proactive conversation with a sustained client, a meeting that can occur face-to-face or on the telephone. Now there is preparation to be done. Table 7.1 provides a list of what you need to know about the client and the business *before* the meeting. You want to be viewed as knowledgeable about the business, skilled in supporting the people-side of business, and well-prepared. You may need to ask your client how to gain access to some items listed in Table 7.1. But it is important to obtain and review documents and information before conducting a proactive conversation.

In addition to the information listed in Table 7.1, it is critical that you prepare a question guide to use in the meeting. Once again, preparing questions to ask is a key factor in conducting a successful meeting. A proactive interview guide is

Table 7.1
Checklist to Prepare for a Proactive Conversation

Obtain as much of the following information as possible prior to conducting a proactive conversation with your client. Check off each item as you obtain it for each specific client.
(✓)

_____ 1. Organization chart for the client's business unit/function.

_____ 2. Most current business plan for the client's business unit/function.

_____ 3. Demographic information regarding the employees within the client's span of control (number of employees by job groups, geographical location of employees).

_____ 4. Information about the product(s) and service(s) provided by the client's business unit/function.

_____ 5. The customers (internal and/or external) for these products and services.

_____ 6. Organizations that directly compete with the business unit/function.

_____ 7. Alliances, joint ventures, acquisitions, and/or divestitures that are occurring and are relevant to the client's organization.

_____ 8. The operational metrics that are used to measure the results from the client's organization—both what they are and the current results against goals.

_____ 9. Other items of relevance such as recent hires, promotions, placement of key people within the division or function.

_____ 10. Suggestion: Send an e-mail to the client with a list of the questions to be discussed in the meeting so your client has an opportunity to prepare his or her thoughts ahead of time.

included in the "Tools" section of this book. You may want to refer to it as we walk through the meeting structure and rationale. You will notice that the Client Profile on the first page of the guide refers to the items listed in Table 7.1.

Introductory Comments

What are your purposes for having this meeting? What do you hope to gain from it? And what are the benefits to the client because you are using some of their valuable time to meet?

These are questions that need to be addressed in your opening remarks. The interview guide provides some sample comments for overviewing the purposes for the discussion. Use these as thought starters for deciding how you will introduce the purposes of your discussion. Also, you want to explain the agenda and confirm the time for the conversation. This way your client knows what to expect during the meeting and can indicate if the original time period is still convenient.

Current Business Goals

This section of the guide provides questions to ask regarding the client's business goals for the current year. An ideal time to have this conversation is when budgets have been finalized and the business plans formed. Another opportune time is when a new client is moving into a position—someone with whom you wish to build a sustained relationship. If you know some of the business goals for the coming year, fill in the guide with that information. In the meeting you can confirm what you understand and change the goals as needed. Of course, you will ask questions about those items where you have limited or no information.

You will notice that SHOULD-IS-CAUSE questions in the guide support the logic contained in the GAPS! Map. This logic and technique is effective in both reactive or proactive conversations.

Something You Can Do

The following are the starter questions contained in the proactive interview guide for each business goal discussed. In this exercise determine for what part of the GAPS! Map each question is seeking information from the client. You may want to refer to the GAPS! Map that appears as Figure 5.2 in Chapter 5 as you do this exercise.

As you decide upon the part of the GAPS! Map where client information most likely will be placed, enter the question number on that part of the map shown in Figure 7.2. When you have completed the exercise, compare your answers to ours, which are shown in Figure 7.3 at the end of this chapter.

Questions Regarding the Business Goal

1. Why is this an important goal at this time? What are the driving forces behind this goal?

2. a) What indicators will be used to measure this goal, and what are the actuals now?

   b) What should be the results at the end of the year?

3. What strategies are being used to accomplish this goal?

4. What forces or factors outside of the organization are going to challenge the achievement of this goal?

5. What about inside the organization? What factors will challenge achievement of this goal?

Questions Regarding Employee Groups

6. Within your department, which employee group(s) will most directly contribute to the achievement of this goal through their performance?

7. a) Considering the business goals and challenges you are facing, what must employees in this group do more, better, or differently if they are to successfully support this goal?

   b) Is there anyone in this group who is currently achieving the operational results you have described as necessary?

   c) If YES, what do they do differently than everyone else?

8. What are the major gaps between what you need employees to be doing on the job to support this business goal and what they are typically doing now?

9. What barriers, if any, challenge employees to perform as needed? What is causing the performance gaps you have identified?

Figure 7.2 The GAPS! Map

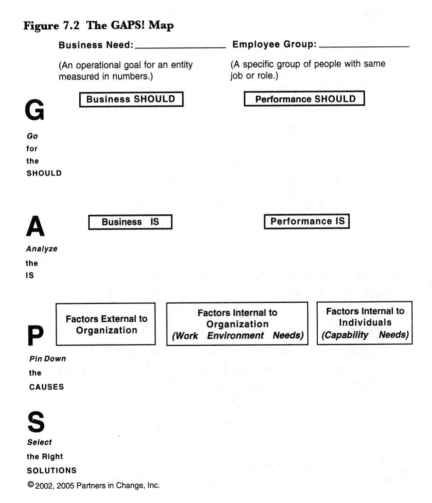

Business Need: _____ Employee Group: _____

(An operational goal for an entity measured in numbers.)   (A specific group of people with same job or role.)

G
Go
for
the
SHOULD

| Business SHOULD | Performance SHOULD |

A
Analyze
the
IS

| Business IS | Performance IS |

P
Pin Down
the
CAUSES

| Factors External to Organization | Factors Internal to Organization *(Work Environment Needs)* | Factors Internal to Individuals *(Capability Needs)* |

S
Select
the Right
SOLUTIONS

© 2002, 2005 Partners in Change, Inc.

In addition to obtaining information regarding current goals, it is also possible to discuss business goals that are more far-reaching in time frame. A section of the guide focuses on goals to be achieved in the next *three* years. Although the logic path is the same as for the current business goals section, you may find that these discussions focus more on strategies and less on specifics. And any opportunities discovered here will almost certainly place you in a very early time frame of a project—just where you want to be!

Managing a Proactive Conversation

When proactive conversations are conducted effectively, they yield deep and insightful information regarding the state of the business for a client. They also are wonderful opportunities to demonstrate to your clients how the Human Resource (HR) function, in general, and you as the SBP, in particular, intend to operate—as a resource that must first understand the business before determining how to support it. This was clearly in evidence when an SBP we know was conducting a proactive conversation with one of her sustained clients. In the conversation they discussed the business needs of the sustained client in depth; virtually no time had been spent with the SBP telling the client about HR services and products he might want to use. Near the close of the conversation, the client acknowledged what a refreshing change it was to "have HR determining what the needs of my business are and how to support them rather than asking me to figure out how I can best use the programs and services offered by HR."

Although these conversations generally are quite successful, there is one potential "go-wrong" that may occur from time to time. Unfortunately, if this "problem" does occur, it will show up at the start of the conversation. The first question you ask in a proactive conversation is for the client to identify a business goal for the coming year. Sounds simple enough! However, some clients will respond with something *other than* a business goal. Without a business goal, it becomes difficult to discuss the follow-up questions. When asking for a business goal, keep in mind that you are seeking an operational objective of the business unit that is measured in numbers. Responses such as "grow market share in the small business market" and "increase subscribers for our service" qualify as business goals. With such a response, the conversation continues as planned.

However, a client may respond with either a business strategy or a performance initiative. A *business strategy* is an overarching plan or method for accomplishing one or more business goals; it is technically a "how" rather than a "what." If a client responds to a business goal question by saying, "We plan to make two acquisitions this year," you have just heard a strategy and not a goal. In this situation you might ask, "For what business purpose are these acquisitions being made?" You may then hear, "To grow market share and revenue," which is a business goal.

What if a client responds to your business goal question by indicating, "We need our employees to be more innovative." You have just heard a performance initiative, not a business goal. Being more innovative is something your client wants employees to do. In this case you can ask the client, "How will being more innovative benefit the business?" You may then hear, "I would expect an increase in the number of new products developed." Now you can ask about specific new product goals and results. So asking the right questions enables you to determine the business goal even when you are first given a business strategy or the performance initiative.

Something You Can Do

Take a moment to determine the type of client response to the question, "What is a business goal for your area in the coming year?"

- For each of the following statements, determine whether it is a business strategy (an overarching "how"), a business goal (the required operational result), or a performance initiative (what people need to do).

- If the statement is *not* a business goal, form a question you might ask to help the client reframe the statement into a business goal.

- To compare your responses with ours, turn to our answers at the end of this chapter.

1. *"I need to reduce operational costs associated with the service side of our business."*

   ____ Business Strategy   ____ Business Goal   ____ Performance Initiative

   If *not* a business goal, what question would you ask to reframe the statement?

2. *"We've got to increase the cross-functionality of our employees. I want them to be capable of working in multiple roles in the production process."*

   ____ Business Strategy   ____ Business Goal   ____ Performance Initiative

   If *not* a business goal, what question would you ask to reframe the statement?

3. *"We will be doing a great deal of product diversification this year; it's important that we do that successfully."*

   ____ Business Strategy   ____ Business Goal   ____ Performance Initiative

   If *not* a business goal, what question would you ask to reframe the statement?

Additional Techniques

You may have heard the story of the explosion and fire that occurred on an oil-drilling platform in the North Sea in 1988. One employee on that rig told the story of being awakened by the explosion and ensuing alarms. Within seconds, this individual ran from his bed and jumped 15 stories down to the water below—water that was so cold he would live but a few minutes if not rescued. He did live to tell the tale, indicating that he made a potentially lethal jump because not to do so meant certain death. And this life-and-death decision was made in an instant. Thus was born the phrase "burning platform," which references any business scenario in which the current state is not an option and there is a sense of urgency to act; in fact, it is imperative to do so (Conner, 1998, p. 118).

Burning platforms offer you an opportunity to work in a proactive manner. Through the relationships you have with your clients, you may learn of a burning-platform situation. By making an appointment to discuss it, you are conducting a variation of the proactive conversation. You will need to modify your approach to focus on the specific business issue for which there is an urgent need to act. This is a targeted—not exploratory—discussion. You can still use many of the questions in the proactive guide found in the "Tools" section of this book. For example, you can ask about the forces and factors impacting the burning-platform situation. You can also ask about the business goals that must be achieved. During the conversation listen for opportunities where you can add value and then offer yourself as a resource for that purpose. Clients with a burning platform are generally most receptive to offers for support.

It is important to view the proactive interview guide as a starter kit of questions. In the meeting you will ask questions based upon the information the client provides. Many of the techniques already discussed in Chapter 6 are certainly relevant in a proactive conversation. For example, drill deeply into information that is vague or unclear. Also, when summarizing information, connect pieces of information to build a holistic view of the situation. And always listen for opportunities where you could ask, "Would it be helpful to . . ."

Another technique is to discuss one business goal at a time. When you focus on a single goal, the information obtained will be richer and clearer. When clients discuss all their goals as one integrated set ("to improve results overall"), the conversation will stay at a high level. You will find it more difficult to gain clarity; identifying opportunities on which to partner is also challenging in this approach.

Make sure that you do not push a project onto a client. The primary purpose of a proactive conversation is to deepen your knowledge of the business. A secondary purpose is to identify a strategic opportunity to support. Clients tend to avoid SBPs who push for a project to work on each time they meet. In this instance your meeting agenda seems to be more for you than for the client!

Closing a Proactive Conversation

Several options are available to you for closing a proactive conversation. The interview guide in the "Tools" section of this book provides four alternatives that can be mixed and matched as appropriate. Are you meeting with a new client for the first time? You may want to use the closing minutes to respond to questions the client has about your role as an SBP and the services you provide. You may also want to seek agreement to meet with the client on a routine basis.

What if your client is managing a business about which you want to learn more? Then you can express that need and ask the client for suggestions on what you might do to build your knowledge of the business. In essence, you are asking the client to coach you in how to learn more about the business of the business. Clients often respond positively to this request. They provide documents, access to people, and wonderful ideas. One client we know offered to provide the SBP with a list of the favorite Web sites he uses to stay current with information about the industry and competitors. He suggested the SBP review these sites on a monthly basis.

Of course, if you have identified a potential project to support, you will be arranging for a follow-up meeting. In this instance, ask your client about background information to review before the meeting. In fact you and your client should agree on any actions to be taken prior to the next meeting.

SBP Tips

1. Proactively identifying strategic opportunities is a critical skill in your role as an SBP. There are several ways to work proactively, one of which is to arrange for meetings with your clients where the agenda is to discuss the client's business goals.

2. The logic contained in the GAPS! Map and the skillful use of SHOULD-IS-CAUSE questions are techniques to use when managing a proactive discussion. The process used in the proactive conversation begins with a focus on business challenges and goals. Next you discuss the performance requirements of employees who significantly contribute to the accomplishment of these business goals. From there you ask about the employees' work environment and capability. The discussion moves down the Need Hierarchy rather than up.

3. By having a proactive conversation with your sustained clients on a routine basis, you are deepening your knowledge of the business and staying current with the concerns of your client. And, in some instances, you will raise questions that result in the client moving ahead with a strategic initiative that, but for this conversation, would not have been identified so soon.

Answers to Something You Can Do

The GAPS! Map in Figure 7.3 shows those parts of the map where information obtained from the questions in the proactive interview guide will most likely be placed. Take a look at the logic. The first five questions focus on the business SHOULD and IS and the factors impacting the business. These questions provide information about the highest need in the Need Hierarchy.

Questions 6 through 9 focus on employee performance and the factors impacting that performance. These questions provide information about the second highest need in the Need Hierarchy.

The interview guide has CAUSE questions for you to ask when you find there is a gap on the business and/or performance side of the map. Note that there are no questions about solutions. This is because it is too early to discuss solutions.

ANSWERS TO SECOND EXERCISE-SOMETHING YOU CAN DO

Our answers to the second *Something You Can Do* exercise are shown here. Let's take a look at each answer.

1. *"I need to reduce operational costs associated with the service side of our business."*

   Our Answer:

   ____ Business Strategy   ✓ Business Goal   ____ Performance Initiative

   This statement refers to the business goal "to reduce operational costs," which is an operational objective of "the service side of our business." The statement does not indicate the number for either the goal or the actual results. Questions 2a and 2b on the interview guide seek that information.

Figure 7.3 GAPS! Map Illustrating Logic of Proactive Interview Questions

Business Need:
What is the business need?

(An operational goal for an entity measured in numbers.)

Employee Group: (6)
What employee group will most contribute to achievement of goal?

(A specific group of people same job or role.)

G

Go
for
the
SHOULD

Business SHOULDs

(2b) What should be the results at the end of the year?

Performance SHOULDs

(7a) What must employees in this group do more, better of differently if they are to successfully support this goal?

(7b) Is there anyone currently achieving optimal results?

(7c) If YES, what do they do differently?

A

Analyze
the
IS

Business IS

(2a) What indicators will be used to measure this goal and what are the actuals now?

Performance IS

(8) What are the major gaps between what you need employees to be doing on-the-job and what they are typically doing now?

Factors External to Organization	Factors Internal to Organization (Work Environment Needs)	Factors Internal to Individuals (Capability Needs)

P

Pin Down
the
CAUSES

(1) Why is this an important goal at this time? What are the driving forces behind this goal?

(4) What forces or factors outside the organization are going to challenge achievement of this goal?

(1) Why is this an important goal at this time? What are the driving forces behind this goal?

(3) What strategies are being used to accomplish this goal?

(5) What about inside the organization? What factors will challenge achievement of this goal?

(9) What barriers, if any, challenge employees to perform as needed?

(9) What barriers, if any, challenge employees to perform as needed?

S *Select* the Right SOLUTIONS

2. *"We've got to increase the cross-functionality of our employees. I want them to be capable of working in multiple roles in the production process."*

   Our Answer:

   ____ Business Strategy   ____ Business Goal   ✓ Performance Initiative

   If *not* a business goal, what question would you ask to reframe the statement?

   "In what way will employees working cross-functionally benefit the business?"

   The client's statement refers to a performance initiative when the client states, "We've got to increase the cross functionality of our employees." To determine if this performance is linked to a business goal, you could ask, "How will increasing the cross-functionality of employees benefit your business?"

3. *"We will be doing a great deal of product diversification this year; it is important that we do that successfully."*

   Our Answer:

   ✓ Business Strategy   ____ Business Goal   ____ Performance Initiative

   If *not* a business goal, what question would you ask to reframe the statement?

   "What business objective is being supported by diversifying our products?"

   The client's statement refers to a business strategy of "doing a great deal of product diversification." A business strategy is a plan or method for accomplishing a business goal. To determine the business goal linked to this strategy, you could ask, "For what business purpose are you doing a great amount of product diversification this year?"

Chapter 8

When the Client Says "YES"

"Opportunities multiply as they are seized."

Sun Tzu (500 B.C.)

Roger, an SBP, learned from the Vice President of Operations
that a task force had just reengineered the supply chain
process in their consumer products company. He also found
out that the new process would require restructuring of two
work groups within Operations. When Roger asked, "Would it
be helpful to determine the best practices required for success
in both of those positions?" the VP answered, "Yes." That
made Roger's day. As he put together a project team, Roger
discovered it was hard to find experienced HR professionals
who could identify the best practices for those positions. The
few who had the required skills could spend only minimal time
on this project. As a result it took four months to complete the
project. When the VP of Operations reviewed the SHOULD
performance for the two positions, he felt that supply chain
managers had developed essentially the same information

over the last few months on their own. The best practices developed by Roger were put on the shelf.

The lesson learned is that when given an important project, you must respond quickly. Line managers want and need the information as soon as possible. They will not value information that arrives weeks after it was needed. In Chapter 3 we said, "When given the opportunity to partner on a major initiative, hit the ground running." When the client says "Yes" to a strategic project, you quickly start implementation by:

- Obtaining reliable information required for project success.

- Selecting and implementing effective solutions.

- Measuring the results obtained by the solutions.

As you begin this chapter, we want to acknowledge that we are providing only an overview of the three SBP activities listed above. Each of these is the focus of numerous books, many of which are included in the "Resources" section of this book. We encourage you to determine your need for additional knowledge and skill as you read this chapter and seek the resources you may require. Let us now take a look at each of these activities.

Obtain Reliable Information Required for Project Success

Reliable information is information that accurately describes the situation. As one business leader said, "Inaccurate information is worse than no information at all." If we inaccurately describe the best practices for a position, the results needed may not be realized. If we inaccurately describe the causes of a performance gap, the solutions implemented will be ineffective.

Considering the need for quick, reliable information, we have found that effective SBPs rely upon a handful of proven assessment approaches. These assessments use straightforward, noncomplex methods and enable fast and accurate analysis. As these methods are used repeatedly by SBPs, their assessment skills are enhanced, the processes streamlined, and reliable information is obtained even more quickly. Actually, there are five assessment approaches you can use for approximately 90 percent of the assessments that focus on human performance. Table 8.1 describes the five assessment options and the overarching question that each answers.

The three types of models provide SHOULD information. The gap analysis focuses on IS information. The cause analysis identifies those factors that make it difficult to apply the SHOULD practices, competencies, and/or work processes on the job. The Information Provided column of Table 8.1 describes the type of information that each assessment yields. The Question Answered column indicates the primary question that each assessment answers; in essence, this forms the purpose statement for the assessment. The Application column lists possible applications for each assessment. The applications are examples of how data can be used; they are not a complete list. As an SBP, you need to be certain of the assessment approach to use. However, we have found that clients are most interested in identifying questions the assessment will answer and agreeing on the applications for the obtained information. Therefore, in discussions with clients, we suggest clarifying what questions will be answered and how the information will be used rather than identifying the name of the assessment needed.

Once you and your clients have decided upon the assessment approach to be used, the next step is to determine sources of information and how that data will be obtained. Table 8.2 provides a list of reliable sources and data collection methods. The best way to obtain SHOULD information is to find individuals within the work group who are achieving the

Table 8.1
Assessment Options

Type of Assessment	Information Provided	Question Answered	Applications
SHOULD Assessments			
Performance Model	Describes performance as it should be if business goals are to be achieved. Generally focuses on a specific job or role.	What must employees in the job do more, better, or differently to achieve the business goals?	• Orientation to job • Role clarity across jobs • Establish performance standards • Coach incumbents • Pay-for-performance compensation systems
Competency Model	Describes skill, knowledge and attributes required for successful performance in support of business goals. Often focuses on a category of employees, such as all first-line supervisors.	What skills, knowledge, and attributes do employees need if they are to perform effectively in support of business goals?	• Recruitment and selection systems • 360° feedback systems • Succession planning • Career planning • Coach incumbents • Performance management systems • Pay-for-skills compensation system
Process Model	Describes the workflow required to accomplish results in support of business goals.	What is the optimal flow of steps or activities to accomplish a specific output or goal?	• Redesign workflow • Establish output goals • Establish input requirements

| | | | • Determine work environment requirements
• Determine staffing requirements |

IS/ACTUAL Assessments

| Gap Analysis | Describes current employee performance, compared to SHOULD performance, identifying both strengths and gaps. | What practices are, and are not, currently being used by employees? | • Identify practices that must change
• Identify practices to reinforce
• Provide focus for areas to probe in a cause analysis
• Identify competencies to enhance and reinforce
• Prioritize where to begin work to enhance performance |

CAUSE Assessments

| Cause Analysis | Identifies factors within the organization and within the employees that are impacting upon desired performance. | What are the reasons for the performance gaps? | • Select appropriate solutions to improve performance
• Identify the organization function to be involved in solution implementation
• Focus resources where greatest return is possible |

Table 8.2
Sources of Data and Data Collection Methods

Assessment Approach	Reliable Data Sources	Reliable Methods of Data Collection
SHOULD Assessments		
Performance, Competency and Process Models	• **STAR Performers** • **Managers of STAR Performers** • Direct Reports of STAR Performers • Customers of STAR Performers • Peers of STAR Performers • Literature[1] • Subject Matter Experts[1] • Internal or External Benchmarking[1]	• Observation • Interview (focus group or one-on-one) • Documentation Review
IS/ACTUAL Assessments		
Gap Analysis	• **Typical Performers** • **Managers of Typical Performers** • Employees of Typical Performers • Customers of Typical Performers • Peers of Typical Performers	• Observation • Interview (one-on-one interviews are preferred) • Questionnaire • Documentation Review
CAUSE Assessments		
Cause Analysis	• **Performers**[2] • Managers of Performers[2]	• Interview (focus group or one-on-one) • Questionnaire • Observation (for tangible barriers/enablers)

BOLD = Source group(s) that should be used if available.

[1]Indicates a reliable source of information where there are no STARs within the client's organization.

[2]Both STAR and typical performers.

job goals and are perceived as being effective. These individuals are often called STARs. There is always a possibility that someone will be identified as a STAR because that person is likeable rather than effective. To avoid this, we encourage you to reach agreement with your clients on the criteria for identifying STARs before selecting any of them. Possible criteria for STARs include individuals who:

- Are meeting or exceeding the operational goals expected of them.

- Are meeting or exceeding the required qualitative goals (e.g., they demonstrate the values of the organization).

- Have been in a position long enough to achieve results over a sustained period of time.

Typically, STAR performers represent no more than 5 percent of the target population. The data collection methods that provide reliable information are those where you interface directly with the STAR performer, such as observation, one-on-one interview, or focus group.

For IS information (also called ACTUAL information), you assess those individuals who are representative of what happens on the job every day. Typical performers are those who are doing the job in a satisfactory manner but are not STARs. The goal is to accurately describe what these individuals typically do on the job. The data collection methods are the same as for the STAR performers, but with one addition—the questionnaire. Questionnaires can be used to obtain ACTUAL performance information when you have a clear description of SHOULD performance. The questionnaire will list the best practices, competency examples, or workflow. The employees, their managers, and others use the scales provided on the questionnaire to compare what typically happens to what SHOULD happen. Table 8.2 lists more sources for SHOULD and ACTUAL information than you would use for any single assessment. The primary sources are shown in bold. If available, they should be used; other sources are used as the client and project require, with one caveat: the greater the number of sources used, the longer the timeline to complete the assessment. Be sure to ask your client if the value of the source is worth the cost in additional time.

For CAUSE information, the most reliable data sources are the performers themselves, both STAR and typical. This is because many causes are not observable and are known only to the performers. Examples are role clarity, recognition, job satisfaction, and access to sufficient information. We have performed numerous cause analyses where the data from employees differed greatly from what their managers indicated. In all cases employees have the clearest picture of factors impacting upon their work. Preferred data collection methods for CAUSE data arc onc-on-one interviews, focus groups, and questionnaires. Direct observation does not work for barriers that are not observable. A nice feature of cause analysis is that it can be combined with obtaining either SHOULD and IS/ACTUAL data; therefore, CAUSE data can be collected with no additional time required for the assessment.

The secret for quick, reliable assessments is to use proven data collection methods and a few reliable data sources. You also want to obtain *only* what is needed to move the project ahead. Avoid the tendency to bundle "nice to know" purposes into an assessment project.

SBP Example

One, Two, Three... Go!

In a large regional bank, the Vice President responsible for back-office operations was concerned about the new operations center. This centralized center was designed to process more transactions per hour and be more efficient than several existing centers that it was replacing.

However, the new center was not reaching its goals. After three months of operation, the number of transactions per hour was still considerably below what had been planned. Additionally, the error rate was three times greater than the goal.

When the VP discussed this situation with Lynn, the SBP, he indicated that it was crucial the situation be turned around. Not only were the operational goals not being met, there were clearly stated procedures that, it appeared, were not being followed. The VP added, "I know that the center has problems. I don't know all the reasons, but I believe the operators need to be better trained." Lynn responded, "I'm sure that we can uncover the reasons. When do you need this information?" The VP said, "By the end of the week." It was already Tuesday morning.

Day One

Lynn used Wednesday to review documentation regarding the operations center. She started with the planning documents that outlined the process, structure, and the requirements for the center. She studied the organization chart, procedures, and reference manuals. She also reviewed the training provided to the operators and their managers.

After a review of the documentation, Lynn phoned the center director to set up time to interview the managers the next morning and to conduct two focus groups in the afternoon.

Day Two

On the morning of day two, Lynn interviewed the operations center director and several managers who were direct reports. These interviews focused on the causes for the gap between what the operators should be doing and what they were currently doing. The management team agreed that the goals and procedures had been clearly defined and that operators had been trained on the procedures. The director and managers also provided their perceptions of some reasons for the operators not handling their jobs as expected. Later that morning Lynn observed some operators at their work stations.

That afternoon Lynn facilitated two focus groups of eight operators. In each focus group the operators agreed they were not able to perform at a satisfactory level. They discussed factors that were barriers to their performance. Lynn asked the focus group members to write on sticky notes the barriers they were encountering, one barrier per sticky note. As these were written, Lynn posted them on a wall chart. She sorted the sticky notes into several categories. When all the information was placed on the wall chart, Lynn summarized the data to the participants to ensure her understanding was accurate.

The observations, interviews, and focus groups provided a great deal of information. People wanted to share what they knew about the problems at the center because they wanted the operations center to be successful.

Day Three

For most of day three, Lynn prepared a report that summarized her findings. While the report acknowledged the shortfall in the operational results, it also described the gaps between the operators SHOULD and ACTUAL on-the-job performance. But the bulk of the report outlined the causes of the performance gaps that Lynn had uncovered over the last two days. The report indicated that several factors dramatically inhibited the operators' ability to perform as well as they should. These factors included:

- Lack of effective coaching by supervisors and managers, who many times gave confusing instructions that differed from the stated procedures required in the new center.

- Lack of a promised Desk Top Reference Manual that had not yet been published and distributed.

- Lack of workspace and functioning equipment that was still being installed.

- Poor lighting and a high level of noise because the construction was not yet complete.

By late afternoon of day three, Lynn and the Vice President were discussing the report about the operations center. Because everyone had agreed that the current performance fell short of the desired performance, the focus of their discussion was squarely on the causes for the performance gaps. By far, the majority of the causes were within the work environment. This provided the VP with the information needed so that he and the operations center director could later agree on solutions. The solutions included ensuring that the supervisors and managers were skillfully coaching the operators to follow the stated procedures. Also, the Desk Top Reference Manual was completed and distributed. In addition, the remaining equipment was installed within a few days, and the construction noise was reduced during the center's primary hours of operation.

On-the-job performance of operators improved as soon as their work environment was enhanced. Operational goals were achieved in six months time. Lynn had hit the ground running on this project, as she delivered an accurate report to her client in three days' time.

Something You Can Do

This exercise provides you with some hands-on experience in selecting the best assessment approach for a given situation. In this exercise three different scenarios are described. Given the information in each scenario, select the one assessment method you feel is most appropriate for the situation and would provide reliable information. Once you have made your selections, turn to the end of this chapter to compare your selection to the assessment approach we would suggest.

- *Situation 1.* A manufacturing organization is preparing to manufacture and launch a complex new product. This product is to be manufactured in several plants throughout the world. It is essential that the product be manufactured in a consistent, high-quality manner. A new position of manufacturing engineer is to be created. Individuals in this job will have a direct impact upon day-to-day manufacturing results. The manufacturing engineers will monitor and adjust the production lines at each plant. The question to be answered is, "What are the practices that will make people in the position of manufacturing engineer successful?" *What type of assessment would you recommend and why?*

- *Situation 2.* A retail organization with several thousand stores in North America is experiencing unusually high turnover of its retail associates. This is surprising because the job itself provides a great deal of satisfaction and the salaries are above average for the industry. Much of the associates' time involves asking questions to determine customers' needs and recommending the appropriate product, which the associate then demonstrates. Management does not know why so many retail associates are leaving the organization. *What type of assessment would you recommend? Why?*

- *Situation 3.* A governmental agency is introducing a new computer technology that will enable it to combine two jobs into one. This is because the computer system will perform many of the functions that are currently completed manually. A position of advisor has been created to operate the new computer system. The system will enable advisors to make recommendations to people who call into the agency with questions and problems more rapidly. The new system requires that the advisors quickly research the person's problem, summarize the information from the computer, and provide the caller with a satisfactory answer. The bureau realizes they need to use different criteria to select people into this position, but are uncertain what these ought to be. *What type of assessment would you recommend and why?*

Select and Implement Effective Solutions

All the reliable data in the world is of little value if you and your client select the wrong solutions. We are reminded of the convenience store chain that was concerned about their stores' ability to achieve revenue and profit goals. They conducted a CAUSE analysis focused on only the store managers' and assistant managers' performance from which they determined that these managers lacked merchandising skills. The SBP and the client implemented merchandising training for the store and assistant managers. The training resulted in a temporary increase in revenue, but several months later it was apparent that it had little long-term impact upon revenue and profit.

What went wrong? They failed to gather information about the work environment. As they learned later, several barriers existed in the work environment, including:

- Corporate buyers were purchasing the merchandise to be sold in the stores; as a result, store managers had little control over the products offered in their stores.

- Minimal information was available to store personnel about the products' benefits to the customer.

- Budget was insufficient to hire "floater" employees to re-stock shelves during promotional events.

The lesson learned is that performance gaps of work groups have multiple root causes. Therefore, multiple solutions are required to close those gaps. Single solutions will not close performance gaps over the long term.

The key to implementing effective solutions is to select effective solutions. You begin by organizing root causes into categories. A CAUSE analysis, whether formal or informal, usually provides a laundry list of causes. To make some sense out of this list, you can organize the causes into the categories of a tool that we call The Gap Zapper. These categories enable you and your client to focus on only those categories where the causes are clustered. There are a couple guidelines to follow when organizing the causes. Make sure the causes are truly root causes, not symptoms. A root cause is a factor for which specific action can be taken to resolve it. When the action is taken, the cause will be eliminated and its effect upon SHOULD performance will be minimized or nonexistent. A symptom, however, is only an indicator of a root cause. Generally, it is difficult to identify solutions for a symptom because symptoms lack specificity. "We lack time to be in the field with customers" is a statement of a symptom. A solution cannot be formed based upon this information. If the statement were, "We lack time to be in the field with customers because of the heavy load of administrative work," a solution to reduce the amount of administrative work in some way can be implemented.

Figure 8.1 illustrates The Gap Zapper with examples of the type of root causes found in each category. The intent of

The Gap Zapper is to clarify the fences between the eight categories of causes. At a macro level there is clear delineation among factors external to the organization, internal to the organization, and internal to the individual. However, for a factor such as "lack of information," a more detailed definition is required. If there is lack of information because the organization's computer and information systems do not have the capability to provide needed information, the category that is focused upon is Systems and Processes. This will result in a solution that focuses on enhancing the system... its hardware, software, and/or programming.

But what if performers do not have access to information that already exists in the information system? In this instance the category to focus upon is Access to Information, People, Tools, and Job Aids. To enhance capability of the information systems would not be a good solution. Rather, we want to focus on how existing information can be communicated to the people who require it. As you can see, without clarity as to root cause, the probability of selecting solutions that will truly close the performance gap is low. Without clarity regarding root causes, we are left to guess as to the solutions required.

Once you have organized the causes by category, the next step is to select solutions that will reduce or eliminate those causes. You begin by identifying possible actions that may diminish the impact of each root cause. In most cases several actions are possible for each root cause. The key is to use an "if... then" approach. For example, *if* "changing expectations of customers" (an external factor) are causing problems, *then* possible solutions may be to (a) modify the marketing and sales strategies and/or (b) adapt the products and services to customer needs. It may also be necessary to conduct a customer analysis to obtain more specific information regarding expectations of customers. Likewise, *if* a "lack of clarity regarding performance expectations and/or standards" (a factor internal to the organization) is a cause, *then* possible solutions may be to (a) establish clear expectations for job results and performance

Figure 8.1 The Gap Zapper with Examples*

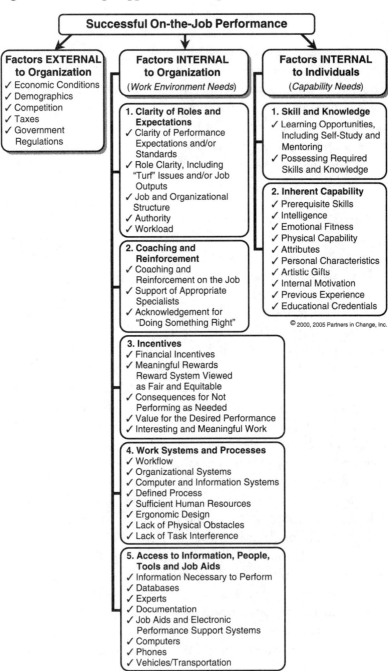

* Examples are stated as enablers to on-the-job performance.

standards, (b) create a SHOULD performance model that describes best practices and criteria for the position and/or (c) have top management communicate their vision, goals, and strategies and how these impact upon individuals in that job. This list of possible solutions can be developed through discussions with STAR performers, their managers, clients, and other stakeholders. Also, a review of the literature and benchmarking can provide additional possible solutions.

Not all solutions are created equal. So how do you judge which solutions will be more effective than others? Harold Stolovitch and Erica Keeps have identified five factors to consider when determining which solutions will be most effective. (1998, p. 113) These factors are:

- *Appropriateness*—The solution addresses a root cause and has a high probability of helping to close the performance gap.

- *Economics*—Funds can be allocated to the solution and a positive ROI is expected from the solution's success.

- *Feasibility*—The organization's capability, resources, and time line can be allocated to this solution.

- *Organizational Acceptability*—The solution is culturally acceptable and will not be rejected because of its nature or characteristics.

- *Individual Performer Acceptability*—The targeted employees can live with the solution.

Each possible solution is rated on these five factors. A sample worksheet for rating the solutions and selecting the most effective solution is included in the "Tools" section of this book. As shown at the bottom of the table, each factor of a possible solution is rated as 0 (unacceptable), 1 (low), 2 (acceptable) or 3 (exceptional). For each possible solution, the ratings of the five factors are added together to provide a total. Those solutions with the highest total have the highest probability of being effective. Any solution with one or more ratings of zero should be rejected. This systematic rating ensures that all solutions will be judged against the same criteria. In addition, it reduces the tendency to select solutions on criteria that are not related to success.

Final decisions about which solutions will be implemented should be made jointly by the business leaders, other stakeholders, and you as the SBP. Obviously, the business leader, with the most to gain or lose from the success or failure of the project, is the final decision maker. But by using this systematic approach, all those involved in making the decision are more likely to support the solutions once they are implemented.

Now it is time to implement the solutions. It has been our experience that SBPs generally do not have a hands-on role in designing and delivering the solutions. Rather, as an SBP you are responsible for clarifying the requirements for implementation of solutions. The first requirement is that the solutions must close the performance gap. The second is that those who design and implement a solution must keep the client informed. So when a solution is selected, you ensure that there is agreement with the client on:

- Expectations of the client and stakeholders.
- Results to be achieved from the solutions.
- Parameters and constraints regarding the solutions.
- Resources required for solution success.
- Communication process for updating the client and stakeholders.

In addition, you will want to remain close to the projects, providing input as needed and ensuring that each solution is moving ahead at a satisfactory rate. Here you work with project managers to ensure that they understand the big picture, including the business and performance needs upon which their solutions have an impact.

You will often become a conduit between the client and the project managers involved in the initiative. You update both the client and the project managers and highlight potential problems that may occur. You work with the client to remove barriers that threaten the effective implementation of a solution. By staying close to both the client and the project managers, you are in a good position to foresee potential barriers. Once these barriers surface, you can work with the project managers to identify the source of the barrier and actions to take to remove it.

As we have said before, we view the SBP role as similar to that of an orchestra leader. The project team members have been selected for their expertise, similar to musicians who are selected for their talents. The project plan is the sheet music. The SBP is the conductor, who ensures that all players follow the plan.

SBP Example

Creating Solutions That Work

Daniel received a request from sales management to provide training for several hundred sales representatives of a large consumer products company. These representatives called upon, and worked with, retail stores. Their responsibility was to increase the volume of their products to those stores and to ensure that the stores successfully implemented product promotions. Sales management requested that the representatives be trained in how to execute advanced spreadsheet functions in order to analyze and interpret the data from sales reports.

Daniel met with sales management to discuss the drivers for the requested training, including what management had observed that indicated training was needed. Management was concerned that the sales representatives were not analyzing and using the sales data to set priorities for product promotions and store visits. However, sales management did agree that it would be helpful if Daniel would gather additional information. In the days that followed, he interviewed STAR sales representatives, typical sales representatives, and their area sales managers. In addition, he reviewed the job descriptions for the sales force and rode with a number of sales representatives as they called upon retail stores. The purpose of this assessment was to determine the SHOULD performance and the IS/ACTUAL performance of both the sales representatives and the area sales managers. This assessment provided some interesting information:

Sales Representatives

- SHOULD: The sales representatives were responsible for executing sales strategies that were created by their area sales managers. The bulk of the sales representatives' time should be spent in the retail stores executing promotions, setting up displays, and promoting the company's brands.

- IS: The sales representatives were being asked to analyze and interpret the sales reports, although that was not a stated job requirement for them.

Area Sales Managers

- SHOULD: The area sales managers were responsible for analyzing the sales report data, providing the sales representatives with strategic direction, including prioritization of store visits, product placement, and promotional activities. In addition, the area sales managers were expected to provide regular constructive coaching to the sales representatives.

- IS: The area sales managers were not analyzing the sales data and were not prioritizing which stores the sales representatives were to visit. In addition, they were not coaching the sales representatives regarding territory and product priorities. Instead of analyzing the sales data, the area sales managers were only sorting the sales reports by territory and forwarding the information to each sales representative.

Sales Planning Team

- SHOULD: A sales planning team at headquarters was responsible for identifying business opportunities and strategies at a national level. This team was expected to provide area sales managers with information that could be used to establish priorities for the territory.

- IS: The sales planning team was providing the area sales managers with reports that were data rich, but difficult to analyze.

The Solutions

When Daniel discussed this assessment and its findings with sales management, several solutions were agreed upon:

- The role of the area sales managers as a coach was reinforced as a key performance requirement. In the future the sales managers would help the sales representatives determine their territory and store priorities. In addition, the sales managers would coach the sales representatives to become more efficient and effective as they interfaced with store personnel and store management.

- All area sales managers were enrolled in a coaching skills workshop where they learned and practiced how to coach sales representatives.

- The sales planning team was asked to restructure the sales report they provided the area sales managers and sales representatives. In doing so, that team created a feature in which each sales representative could enter a territory code, which then produced a report listing the stores within the territory. This report automatically recognized key trends occurring within each territory. Area sales managers used this report and coached the sales representatives on how to address the trends.

- Daniel created a self-guided manual for the sales representatives, enabling them to more effectively use the sales reports and the automated spreadsheet functions.

The Results

Several hundred sales representatives and approximately 50 area sales managers reduced their weekly administrative time by many hours. Daniel's efforts also resulted in the learning organization not delivering advanced spreadsheet training to several hundred sales representatives, which was the original request. Clearly the original request would have required substantial resources, while providing minimal results. The sales representatives were now more available to work directly with retailers. The area sales managers were now coaching the sales representatives more effectively. Several months later, sales management indicated that these solutions were one of three contributing factors that led to record-breaking sales for the fiscal year.

Measure the Results Obtained by the Solutions

We are all familiar with the expression, "The operation was a success, but the patient died." A business analogy to this would be, "The training was a success, but there was no change in on-the-job performance." Or maybe, "The new sales compensation package was well received, but there was no increase in revenue."

To make sure that implemented solutions do provide results, you can measure the effect of solutions on the original performance and business problem. Two purposes for measuring the impact of solutions are:

- To determine whether or not the expected results were achieved.

- To identify actions that must be taken to maintain or increase the results already achieved.

When measuring results, you want to obtain an accurate picture of what has actually occurred as a result of the solutions. Otherwise, you may draw erroneous conclusions regarding any subsequent steps to be taken. We have encountered situations where the solution implemented was measured and deemed successful, but there was little or no change in on-the-job behavior. We also have encountered situations in which the business results improved, but the solutions were not measured to determine to what degree they contributed to the achievement of these results.

Good measurement begins by determining the purposes for the measurement. In essence, these are the overarching questions that clarify the intent of measurement activities. In this way, measurement design is similar to how you determine the type of assessment to be used—you determine the major questions you wish to answer from the data you are about to obtain. There are four overarching questions that are typically addressed through a measurement initiative.

1. *Did each solution produce the intended results?* Each solution utilized will have unique intended results. For example, a learning solution is best measured by determining the amount of learning that has occurred. Therefore, if the solution involved developing consultative selling skills for sales associates, a viable approach would be to measure the skill level of sales associates after the training is completed. To what degree did skills increase? And are the skills to the level required for job success? If the solution involves developing a process to improve talent retention, an effective measure could be to pilot the talent retention process, determining whether it accomplishes what was intended.

2. *Did the on-the-job performance change as expected? If performance change does not occur, what are the reasons?* The key here is to have identified what on-the-job performance is desired and should be measured before implementing solutions. In this way measurement is a front-end process—you must know the results you seek before you begin to measure. You typically want to measure the desired performance both before and after the solutions are implemented. By doing this you can identify the degree of change that occurs. With the sales associates you could measure the frequency with which they are using the consultative selling techniques with their customers and prospects both before and following training. In the talent retention situation, you might assess the degree to which managers, who are expected to use the talent retention process, are doing so. In each instance you also want to determine why people are not using the skills or process as intended. This is information that you use to determine what corrective actions to take.

3. *Were the desired business results achieved, and if results did not occur, what are the reasons?* The key here is to define the expected business results to be achieved because of the solutions. As the solutions are implemented, the actual results can be

tracked and trends can be identified. For the sales associates, you may decide to track changes in sales revenue, the size of initial orders, and customer satisfaction. In the talent retention situation, you could track the retention percentage for the targeted employees and their level of job satisfaction. Again, you also want to determine causes for any lack of success that occurs.

4. *Were the clients satisfied with the results achieved and the manner in which the work was done?* Here the focus is on the client's satisfaction with, and their reaction to, the solutions and how they were implemented. As with the three previous questions, the key is to identify the expectations of clients for solutions and their implementation first. Then you can determine the type of information that is needed. For some client expectations, you may use numeric measures. For other client expectations, a more qualitative type of information could be required. To determine client satisfaction, you might ask about their level of satisfaction with the:

- Amount of change in the on-the-job performance obtained.

- Amount of change in business results.

- Specific solutions that were implemented.

- Implementation strategy that was used.

- Manner in which the project managers interfaced with the clients and kept the clients informed.

- Reactions of the work groups impacted by the solutions.

Clearly, the critical elements of measurement are to determine the overarching questions, or measurement purposes, and to identify the expected results. Once you and your client reach an agreement on the overarching questions, the data collection and analysis become relatively straightforward. The guidelines that were mentioned earlier in this chapter about data sources and data collection methods still apply. Select data sources that can provide accurate information, use multiple data sources so you can verify how reliable the information is, and use straightforward, noncomplex data collection methods. By following these guidelines, you will be able to efficiently collect reliable information. As an SBP, your role may be similar to what we have discussed before. That is, you will orchestrate the data collection and measurement process rather than actually do the data collection. Designing data collection tools, gathering the information, and tabulating the data are best done by individuals with that expertise. The benefit of using experienced individuals is that they can typically complete a project more efficiently and reliably, avoiding the many pitfalls inherent to data collection and measurement. This also provides you with time to continue identifying and working on other strategic projects.

Once the data has been collected and analyzed, you play a key role in discussing the results with your client. This means you must be very familiar with the measurement results and what those results indicate about the effectiveness of the solutions. You must be clear as to what factors helped to make the solutions successful and those factors that were barriers to success. When the measurement results are discussed with the client, you wear two hats—one hat as an objective evaluator of project results and another as a facilitator of discussions about the measurement information. As the objective evaluator of results, you present the conclusions derived from the data. Conclusions are deductions that have been reached after examining the specific results obtained. An example is with the sales associate situation mentioned earlier. We measured this situation, and the data results led to the conclusion that for those sales associates where the sales managers provided coaching, the sales associates applied the consultative selling techniques more effectively. When coaching did not occur, there was limited performance change. Another conclusion was that the sales revenue of the sales associates who received coaching increased by 18 percent over last year, while the sales revenue of sales associates who were not coached increased only 6 percent.

As the meeting facilitator, you want to stimulate discussion regarding actions that should now be taken. This includes actions to ensure that improvement already achieved is maintained as well as actions to address barriers to success. The clients typically initiate lively discussions about actions that should be taken to improve those areas where results were less than expected. Your role is to be a resource and provide input, while keeping the discussion focused.

Implementation "Go Wrongs"

Certainly, when supporting a strategic project, Murphy's Law can raise havoc with even the best-laid plans. Let us take a look at some common "go wrongs" that we have both seen and experienced.

- *Your client loses interest in the solutions being implemented.* When this occurs, you need to engage the client in a discussion about the original problem; you also need to raise the question of whether work on the solutions should continue. At this time you can also probe to determine the reasons for the client's loss of interest. This often uncovers concerns about the solution design and/or how the solutions are being implemented. Once these concerns are uncovered, you need to acknowledge and address them, determining whether the solutions should be implemented, modified, or halted.

- *Your original client is transferred and a new client is appointed.* Now you need to initiate a meeting with the new client to determine where this project fits into this client's priorities. You and the client discuss whether or not the client feels that work on the solutions should continue. If it should continue, you can then clarify any changes needed as well as the resources required. If the work on solutions is to stop, you and the client should agree on the message to be communicated to stakeholders and who will communicate that message.

• *Your client wants to implement only a single solution that will be insufficient to yield desired results.* In this case you need to indicate that the solution, by itself, will impact only one root cause; the other root causes will limit results that can be obtained. This is essentially the "push back" behavior we described in Chapter 6. You might also consider a "yes, and" approach. You do that by indicating that the solution the client suggests can be implemented and suggest other solutions or actions to take at the same time to complement this client's solution.

• *The project is taking too long, and your client is growing dissatisfied.* Here you need to determine the causes for the delay. You and the project managers should meet with the client and discuss progress to date, future actions to take, and any potential roadblocks. At this time the group can agree on actions needed to remove any roadblocks and form an action plan to ensure that the pace of implementation increases.

SBP Tips

1. When given an important project, you must hit the ground running. Line managers expect quick action. If they must wait weeks for something they need right away, they will have little motivation to partner on the project.

2. Move quickly to obtain information needed about what should be happening, what is happening, and the causes for the gaps. Obtain only that information that is unknown and required. You discuss this information in a facilitated meeting with your client, agreeing on the solutions to be implemented.

3. The first step of implementation is to organize causes into categories, then select and implement appropriate solutions. The key here is to keep solutions simple. Complex solutions slow down the project and have a greater number of problems. Make sure that your solutions include some "low-hanging fruit." Determine the minimum actions needed to obtain results. In other words, do a few things well.

4. Measure the effectiveness of the solutions. Good measurement defines the contribution solutions had on the results achieved. It also lets you know what actions are needed to maintain or increase the results already achieved. By taking actions, if needed, you ensure that results are sustained over time.

Answers to Something You Can Do

*   *Situation 1—Manufacturing Organization.* **Our answer is to use a performance model.** Because clients want to know what practices should be used by a manufacturing manager, we recommend a performance model to describe the best practices required for success in that specific job.

*   *Situation 2—Retail Organization.* **Our answer is a cause analysis.** Because management wants to know why so many retail associates are leaving the organization, we recommend a cause analysis to identify the reasons for associates leaving the retail stores.

*   *Situation 3—Governmental Agency.* **Our answer is to use a competency model.** Because the bureau wants to know what criteria to use for selecting advisors, we recommend a competency model to describe the skills, knowledge, and attributes required to perform effectively as an advisor. These competencies can then be designed into a recruitment and solution process.

PART FOUR

INFLUENCING BUSINESS STRATEGIES AND DIRECTION

Figure P4.1 Strategic Business Partner Accountabilities

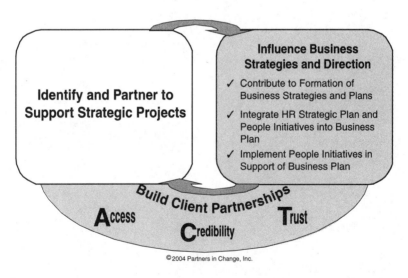

©2004 Partners in Change, Inc.

Working on strategic projects with clients is a key Strategic Business Partner (SBP) role, and for many this will be the primary focus for their work. For some SBPs, however, their role will expand to include focusing on enterprise-wide requirements. When operating at the table in this manner, you are not so much focused on individual initiatives; rather, you are forming and supporting future strategic business directions that will guide the organization for some years. Does the organization need to grow marketshare in Asia? What is required to make that happen from a Human Resources (HR) perspective? Should the organization divest itself of a specific product line? What must be done to ensure that this action occurs with a minimum of "pain" to the people affected, including employees, customers, and shareholders? The questions that SBPs help to address when "at the table" are discussed in Chapter 9.

Finally, what must an HR function do to successfully embrace a more strategic role and to support those individuals who work as SBPs? The changes can be significant in terms of the function's work process and structure as well as for the capability required of team members. These factors are discussed in Chapter 10.

Chapter 9

Being at the Table

"The best way to predict the future is to create it."

Peter Drucker

The phrase *at the table* is used with increasing frequency; perhaps it is an overused term. But what does it mean when an SBP is working at this level with clients? Moreover, how is it different from the work described in the previous section of this book? Let us discuss these questions before moving more deeply into what SBPs actually do when they work in this manner.

Once you have developed client relationships based upon access, credibility, and trust, you are in a position to identify and partner with clients on specific strategic initiatives and projects. These projects often focus on goals for the next one or two years; these are typically goals for a business unit such as sales, marketing, operations, or finance. By contrast, when at the table, you will focus on needs that are addressing a large portion of the organization and are often enterprise-wide. The view is long term—looking forward as much as three to ten years. The nature of this work means there will be ambiguity for some period of time during which focus is not so much on solutions as it is on correctly identifying the problem or opportunity to be addressed. Once the problem is clarified, large-scale strategies and plans are discussed and established. Because of the comprehensive nature of this work, there are a myriad of issues to consider. At some point in the work, specific projects and initiatives will be identified. In this manner, the work that is done at the table helps to set an agenda and establish priorities for the HR function. As an SBP you will generally have a role in executing those initiatives that focus on preparing people and the organization to move ahead.

Not every SBP can, or should, be working at this level. After all, how many people who specialize in the human side of business are required when forming strategic and business plans for an organization? Most organizations need a voice to represent this perspective—not a chorus! In addition, moving to this level is something an SBP *earns* the right to do. We value Wayne Brockbank's perspective on this point when he said:

> "Earning that place at the table is a function of many factors including knowing the strategy, culture, vocabulary, and operating issues of the business, having passion for issues which add greatest value to external customers and shareholders, and focusing on financial results." (1997, p. 66)

The phrase *at the table* connotes formality, as though this type of work is completed in meetings with leaders around a conference table using a formal process with documented results. In actuality, the type of contribution and influence we are describing is organic, iterative, and ongoing. Yes, some formal meetings *do* occur; but much of this work is done when meeting informally with leaders or in conversations over a working lunch. After all, organizations are dynamic, with change a constant. What if the economy has suddenly become robust in a market that was anticipated to be flat during the annual strategic planning process? You want to respond, and respond quickly.

SBPs who are at the table work strategically with business leaders in three ways. Specifically, they:

- Contribute to the formation of business strategies and plans.
- Integrate the HR strategic plan and initiatives to the business plan.
- Implement people initiatives in support of the business plan.

Contribute to Formation of Business Strategies and Plans

Just imagine the types of discussions that must have occurred early in the life of Starbucks as that organization's leaders dialogued how to position the business model from selling coffee, a commodity product, to selling an experience. Consider the implications of that decision for all facets of the organization, including the performance requirements for associates and the organizational support needed. Numerous examples abound in the business press:

- Hewlett Packard and Compaq as they made a decision to merge.
- JetBlue Airways as the organization moved into the low-cost airline market.
- Toyota's decision to build and support manufacturing facilities in North America.

For any organization, there are times when they are forging a revised or completely new strategic intent and business plan. SBPs who are at the table are part of these discussions and the decision making that is done.

Some of the processes and capabilities already discussed in this book are viable and needed when at the table. Certainly deep knowledge of the business will be a prerequisite. Asking thought-provoking questions will continue to be vital. The SHOULD-IS-CAUSE logic that we have previously described is relevant. Asking questions such as, "What business are we in—and what business SHOULD we be in?" evidence application of that logic path, albeit at a broader level.

Now let's look at some of the differences when you are working at the table with business leaders.

Knowledge and Use of an Organizational Architecture Model

The GAPS! Map is a way of organizing information about a specific business need and the day-to-day performance required from one or more employee groups. When at the table looking at a wider scope, it is still vital to be able to "chunk" information. In essence, you and the organization's leaders must helicopter above the organization to view the many elements that are affected by the business decisions made. An organizational architecture model is a tool for identifying those elements being impacted by a major decision. Frequently SBPs are the individuals who propose the model to be used in the organization. There are many models that have been validated and affirmed, including the models of Jay Galbraith, Geary Rummler, and David Nadler. These models generally contain organizational elements such as rewards, structure, culture/norms, strategy, processes, and people (including capability). The specific model used is not the issue. What is vital is to have a model that is valid and resonates with your organization's leaders.

Knowledge of the Organization's Strategic and Business Planning Processes

Like architectural models, there are many strategic planning processes used in organizations today. As an SBP who is at the table, you must be knowledgeable regarding the strategic and business planning processes utilized in your organization. There are common elements to most strategic planning processes, including a situational or environmental analysis, formation of assumptions, creation of a vision, mission, goals, and strategies, as well as the risks associated with decisions made. When at the table, you will be contributing content that is relevant to the strategic and business plans; you may even be asked to facilitate discussions using the process. You want to offer your observations when the team is deviating from the process. For all these reasons, knowledge of the strategic and business planning processes used by leaders in your organization is a requirement.

Something You Can Do

Do you know what organizational architecture model is used in your organization? Do you know what strategic planning and business planning processes are being used? As an SBP, it is critical to have knowledge of these. Here are some questions you may want to answer for your organization.

Organizational Architecture Model

1. What is the organizational architecture model? What components are contained in it?

2. If there is a model, but you are uncertain as to its content, who can you meet with to develop a deeper knowledge of it?

3. Should you find that there is no accepted organizational architecture model, what is the level of perceived value to forming one? What role can you have in that effort?

Strategic and Business Planning Processes

1. a) What are the strategic and business planning processes utilized in your organization?

   b) What actions do you need to take to grow your knowledge of these processes?

2. What individuals are viewed as the owners of each process?

3. Should you find that there is no accepted strategic planning and/or business planning process, what is the level of perceived value in adopting one? What role can you play in that effort?

Be a Dot Connector, Thinking Outside Your Area of Responsibility

We have mentioned previously that it is important to link together what appear to be disparate pieces of information. In this way, you see patterns and themes in discussions and identify connections that may not be obvious. You are taking the skill of reframing to a higher level, helping to view problems from new angles. We recall the remark of an SBP who said,

"When working at the table, you must have your fingers in many pots, helping to tie the pieces together."

It is also critical to think and work as a businessperson, not only as an HR professional. Obviously, it is important to avoid HR-speak; the terms *intervention* or *pedagogy* are not used. In essence, you work from the perspective of the proverbial 30,000-foot level. You view the entire landscape, seeing connections and potential conflicts rather than focus on any single element. You are not representing the HR function so much as you are contributing to business strategy with a keen eye on the people implications of the proposed business plans.

There are a few additional requirements for success in this role.

- *Be Courageous and Speak with Candor.* Decisions made at this level will influence the business and guide its decisions for years to come. Therefore, each person—including the SBP—must contribute. This means asking the "dumb" questions as well as bringing the elephant in the room that is not being addressed to everyone's attention. One SBP we know refers to this type of communication as providing clients with a "leadership moment." When the SBP hears of potential disconnects or discontent in the organization regarding an initiative or business goal, he informs his client, the Chief Operating Officer (COO), of the situation. He encourages the COO to discuss and address the issues that are below the surface yet critical to business success.

- *Disagree Privately and Agree Publicly.* When at the table, it is important to discuss concerns and clarify disagreements. Sometimes you will support a solution that others at the table will not support. But once a decision is made, you must publicly and personally support that initiative, doing all that is necessary to ensure its success.

SBP Example

Forming Business Strategies

Cam works in a large petroleum organization. One of his clients is the Vice President (VP) of Refining and Supply with the *downstream business*. In a petroleum organization, downstream business is all the work and products that move oil from crude to cash. In this organization downstream was a smaller part of the business, yet it had a large amount of potential. A goal was established by the president of this business to move from the second-largest player in this market to become number one. All vice presidents were tasked to identify how much additional operating revenue (profit) could be obtained beyond that already committed to in the business plan. VPs were then to form and execute plans against those targets.

The VP of Refining and Supply had a goal of generating $150 million additional profit into the business than originally planned. That goal was the given—everything else was up for discussion. This is where Cam entered. He used an architectural model that included nine unique elements such as strategy, process, structure, goals, and consequences. Cam engaged the VP in numerous discussions to assess the current state of the organization against the requirements of this model relative to the goal they were supporting. Data were obtained from multiple people and sources and then synthesized and discussed by the VP and Cam. Through these discussions, Cam did several things that the VP acknowledged were helpful:

- Pushed the VP beyond his comfort zone to realize that this goal required a transformational change of the Refining and Supply organization. The set of solutions needed would be complex and multiple.

- Helped the VP realize the leadership gap that existed between his current leadership style and practices and what would be required to mobilize and execute resources for this daunting goal.
- Worked with the VP to identify the people and resources that could best work on the required initiatives.

Once there was some degree of focus as to what was required, the VP recruited key members of his team to take the planning to the next level. In this stage of work, Cam facilitated the meetings. Five project teams were launched and worked over a period of nine months. Cam's primary role during this time was to (a) continue working in an advisory role to the VP and to (b) ensure teams were interconnected and not working on parallel or unintegrated paths. The challenge was to keep focus on the collective goal and not on any single solution within it. Cam also coached the VP to continue to ask the teams, "What worries you regarding the sustainability of your proposed solution? Solutions need to have lasting effects and be valid beyond the initial effort."

The result? The VP and his team did achieve the $150 million goal in the time frame needed. The VP clearly viewed Cam's assistance as key to the successful effort. This VP acknowledged that Cam "had answers to important questions I didn't even know I had" and "was a truth seeker, sharing those truths with me no matter how he thought I would respond, taking me out of my comfort zone when needed."

Integrate HR Strategic Plan and Initiatives into Business Plan

"Based upon where the business needs to go in the next five years, what are the key requirements and priorities for HR as it supports these goals?"

This question indicates that the results of discussions to form the business strategy and plan are the *inputs* to this SBP accountability. Once in this phase of work, the Need Hierarchy that we discussed in Chapter 1 becomes relevant. More than at any other time while working with the organization's leaders, SBPs are now translating business needs into performance and workplace requirements. What if the business need is to implement a new distribution channel into the marketplace? Which jobs within the organization will be most critical to successful execution of that goal? What will people in those jobs need to do more, better, and/or differently? What supports, in terms of both the work environment and capability enhancement, will be required so these individuals can fulfill these expectations? Answers to these questions will help set the HR agenda and priorities.

When working at this level as an SBP, you employ a strategic planning process for HR that is aligned with the strategic process used by the business. You also need to be skillful in designing and guiding organizational change initiatives. So what are some of the important requirements for SBPs when integrating HR's strategic plan to the plan for the business? There are five that we want to mention.

1. *Communication of Business Plan to HR Colleagues.* You are the link between the business leaders, who have forged and are ultimately accountable for the success of the plan, and the people within HR whose work priorities need to align with this plan. It is vital that the HR staff understand the plan, the rationale behind it, and the implications of that plan for the work they will be doing. A March 2002 study conducted by Gallup Management Journal indicates that only 31 percent of workers within the U.S. believe they are helping their company to achieve enterprise-wide business goals. (Adkins, p. 30) Your role is truly to ensure that HR employees understand the link between an HR initiative and the requirements of the business.

2. *Organizational Audits to Identify Readiness.* We indicated earlier in this chapter the need for you to work from an organization architecture model. That model now will be the guide for any assessment work that may be required. What if your organization has determined that it will be actively seeking to acquire another firm in order to broaden its market reach and be more of a global player? Some people, who also work at the table, will be involved in activities associated with the due diligence required to determine one or more suitable candidates for this merger. Meanwhile you can be determining the organization's readiness to successfully integrate an acquired firm into the mix. This is the reason for an organizational audit. Given what a successful acquisition requires (the SHOULD), what IS the current state in terms of work process? Structure? People receptivity and capability? Typically, an organizational audit will assess the current state in some or all of the elements contained within the organization's architectural model. Your role is to identify both the strengths and potential flat sides of the organization, proposing initiatives to close any identified gaps.

3. *Propose Initiatives and Solutions That Ensure Alignment of People with Business Requirements.* For an organization to succeed, there must be alignment between what the business requires and what people do from day to day; of course, to obtain this level of performance requires a supportive work environment and capable people who are tasked to do the work. Perhaps an organization has determined that to remain competitive, it *must* support an entrepreneurial culture with innovation in virtually all facets of the business—from product development through order fulfillment. This requires that people perform differently—with more outside-the-box thinking and experimentation. However, in this organization, there is no variable pay system and bonuses are paid only to the top tier of management. Also, the cultural norms are such that people feel

more punished for failure than rewarded for success. Clearly, the entire system of consequences—tangible and intangible—is out of alignment with the requirements of the business. SBPs must identify this type of nonalignment and work with leaders to change it. One way is to ask the right questions and to propose solutions. For example, given what the business needs to do, should the organization be flattened? Are new roles or work teams required? Maybe the structure should change so that employees are organized around process and not around function. These are the types of issues that you discuss when at the table. In addition, you must be prepared to offer solutions.

4. *Provide the Business Case for HR Solutions That Are Proposed.* Given a strategic goal for the organization, it is important to ask what type of talent will be required to ensure success. And, given the answer to that question, you then need to determine if that talent should be (a) recruited from the outside, (b) promoted from within, or (c) a combination of those options. Perhaps some of the work involved would best be outsourced to an external supplier. All possible solutions ought to be considered. Part of this consideration includes analysis of the business and financial case for each option. For the business, what are the upsides, as well as downside risks, that go with each option? What is the cost and potential return of each option? What is your recommendation, given the above considerations, for how to proceed? These are the types of questions that leaders expect of you when you are working with them at the table.

5. *Knowledge of HR Staff's Capability.* When proposing solutions, you will be suggesting the resources to be applied to these solutions. It is imperative to have a realistic assessment of the internal capabilities and readiness of HR staff members. Your credibility will be reduced if you overcommit and under-deliver.

SBP Example

Aligning HR Plans to Requirements of the Business

Kevin works in a food service company with thousands of stores globally and three major brands, each with its own growth goals and challenges. The majority of the stores are owned by franchisees. Kevin leads the learning and performance function for this organization and is very much at the table with the leadership team when business goals and strategies are formed. Once the three-to-five-year plan has been developed for the organization (done on an annual basis), Kevin works to ensure alignment between the goals and priorities of his function and the requirements of the business. The following are some of the major tactics he uses to ensure this alignment is developed.

- *Form initiatives that are then proposed to his clients.* This process requires communicating the big picture for the business to his team of 36 people. Kevin forms a straw dog of possible initiatives that will support the business goals and passes this proposed list by (a) his direct reports, (b) brand teams, and (c) franchisees. He is seeking both affirmations of the draft initiatives as well as other suggestions. With the input from others, a final proposed plan is taken forward to the Chief Operating Officer and other leaders for final approval. In this way Kevin is developing plans with his team that are more likely to be (a) appropriate and (b) yield support from team members whose engagement is required for success. This process requires approximately 90 days to complete, with a goal of being finalized when the new fiscal year commences.

- *Provide the business case for a solution under consideration.* It is common for the solutions proposed to require a financial investment. Kevin is skilled at developing and communicating the business case for the investment. Consider the time Kevin proposed investment in an on-line learning system as one initiative to support a business goal of differentiating the brand in a very competitive marketplace. This involved a substantial capital investment in hardware that would need to be placed into each of the stores. Kevin provided the numbers regarding the savings in tuition and travel costs as well as the opportunity to develop 100 percent of the 150,000 employees in the company annually, not just the 10 percent now being reached. This proposed on-line learning system would enable the company to realize a long-held goal—that of certifying store employees. The system could accommodate on-line testing and would move the organization toward differentiation in the marketplace as employees evidenced greater skill, product knowledge, food safety focus, and customer service. Leaders adapted the proposed plan, and both the on-line learning system and certification process are in effect today.

- *Continually communicate to and with the HR team.* Once the plans are rolling, it is vital to keep the HR team current with the status of these projects. The needs of the business will change as the year progresses. Kevin ensures that communication flows both to and from the members of his department by implementing a structured communication process that includes:

  - An annual meeting at the start of the year.
  - Quarterly meetings with his direct reports.

- Weekly meetings of the various project teams.

Kevin leads the first two meetings and participates in as many of the weekly meetings as possible. This commitment to communication ensures that members of the learning and performance organization are kept current as to needs of the business and that Kevin will be up to date on the progress of the ongoing initiatives.

Implement People Initiatives in Support of the Business Plan

It's often been said that most strategies fail not from insufficient planning but because of poor execution. As Lawler and Mohrman indicate, "Execution failures are often the result of poor human capital management. This opens the door for HR to add important value if it can deliver change strategies, plans, and thinking that aid in the development and execution of a business strategy," (2003, pp. 2–3).

Once into the implementation phase of work, there are many roles for you—as the SBP—to fill, including:

- *Project Manager.* All people initiatives, whether redesigning a rewards system or developing people in certain job groups, will generate their own project task list. As an SBP, you can help to orchestrate and align HR resources against these various initiatives. Then you need to work in the role of a macro-project manager, ensuring that these initiatives are operating as intended. When there are roadblocks or problems encountered, you will be a primary resource to help resolve these issues.

- *Broker of Resources.* SBPs have told us that one of the primary value-adds they bring at this stage is the knowledge of people with whom to contract for specific needs and services. To return to our earlier analogy, the SBP is a type of orchestra conductor—identifying and engaging those who will be a part of the orchestra of resources needed to implement the initiatives and helping to ensure that all resources are working from the same sheet of music. Sometimes the required resources will reside within the organization; other times it will be necessary to look outside the organization for this support. If one of the initiatives is to develop salespeople in strategic account management, what external resource will you bring into the organization to work with you and the clients? This is where having a network of contacts can be most helpful.

- *Link between Clients and Those Who Are Implementing Initiatives.* As an SBP, you are the linchpin between your clients and those who are working to support the client's initiatives. Communication will of course be key. Rarely do projects run into difficulties due to too much communication; typically, the reverse is the problem. Communication can take many forms: formal update meetings, e-mail messages, and phone contacts. It is vital is that you design a communication process that keeps the clients and those who are working on the various projects updated and engaged. The result is a group of project teams that together produce results that no single individual or team could produce.

- *Keeping Focus on Execution of Plan.* Because initiatives are generally occurring over a period of months, there is a need to ensure people remain linked and committed to achievement of the ultimate goals. Sometimes it is important to re-engage those individuals who are implementing the various solutions; other times it will be necessary to meet with clients who may not have filled their commitments to the initiative. Without focus on a sustained basis, these initiatives can die of benign neglect. It is better to make a conscious and thoughtful decision that the priorities are shifting and the initiative will no longer be a focus. Bottom line: If you detect that your clients are beginning to ignore the initiative, it is important to bring this to their attention and discuss how to proceed.

Accountability and Measurement of Results

A vital part of the implementation phase is the monitoring and measurement of results that are being obtained. Results of interest to you and your clients are (a) performance change that is occurring for the employees whose role is shifting, (b) results regarding the changes made to the work environment infrastructure and the capability of employees, and (c) results that are occurring in the operational metrics and business goals that were the drivers for the initiatives in the first place. As an SBP, you need to agree with your clients at the beginning of implementation on what results are expected and how these will be measured.

Many SBPs use a balanced-scorecard approach for measurement. They determine the key result *categories* that need to be included. An organization with whom we worked implemented a major initiative designed to enhance efficiency in its global manufacturing operations. The result categories they focused upon were:

- Achievement of operational metrics for manufacturing operations.

- Efficiency of the processes used to design and implement the solutions that were utilized.

- Customer satisfaction with the quality of product that was produced and delivered.

- Success in how employees performed, as they were now required to work in cross-functional teams.

Metrics and ways of measuring were designed for each of these four result categories. Achievement of operational metrics, by itself, was insufficient. What was vital was a balanced set of results that included customer satisfaction with products produced, efficiency of operation, and employee performance. The combination of the results from all areas was critical.

One other item to note: It is vital that as an SBP you accept joint accountability with your clients for the results that are obtained. It is not just that a new organizational structure was designed and implemented, but that the desired business and performance results also occurred. We know an SBP who retained the services of an external consultant to work on an enterprise-wide initiative, with the clients paying the fees involved. Unfortunately, the results from this consultant's work were less than acceptable, resulting in the termination of this consultant's services and the need to bring in another resource. This time the SBP's budget paid the fees involved, clearly evidencing some accountability for the lack of success with the initial selection.

At the same time, it is vital that you clarify the fences between what is your accountability as an SBP and what is the accountability for the clients you are supporting. To the organization, all initiatives need to be viewed as emanating from the clients; it is deadly when work is labeled as an "HR initiative" by the population at large. Therefore, a critical client role is to communicate the business case for the initiatives and the expectations that leaders have of others regarding the initiative. It is the clients who should communicate these messages. Clients also need to step in and take action when resistance begins to surface. As an SBP you do *not* want to assume roles and responsibilities that are truly those of the client. We certainly support what Chris Rolfe, a VP of Human Resources, said in Bossidy and Charan's book, *Execution*. "HR can build all these elaborate systems, but it takes the leader of the company to make it real," (2002, p. 175).

A Special Note to the Corporate SBP

One of the roles for SBPs who work at the corporate level is to assist and support their HR colleagues in the field who will be doing much of the implementation work. While corporate often determines the goals and strategies for HR, there needs to be some flexibility regarding how the initiative will be managed in various field locations—this is particularly true if these locations are throughout the world. As a corporate SBP, you must have in-depth understanding of the strategic initiatives and how they link to the business needs. This is information that you need to share with your HR colleagues who are expected to fully support the rollout of initiatives in field locations. However, there is an inherent source of conflict in this rollout process. Corporate HR seeks consistency throughout the enterprise in how the solutions are used on the job and how initiatives are implemented. Additionally, corporate HR seeks business unit data that can be rolled up into a corporate report. By contrast, business units want flexibility to modify the initiative to their unique environment and to implement the initiative without difficulties and administrative requests that require a great deal of staff time.

So as a corporate SBP, what can you do to ensure a win for both the corporate and business unit organizations? You can brief the business unit leaders, HR leadership, and SBPs within the business units early in the planning for the new initiative. You want everyone to understand the need for the initiative and its benefits for the enterprise *and* the business units. Early in the planning process, meet with your counterparts in the business units and contract with them regarding their needs for input to the initiative as well as how they wish to be kept informed during the planning, design, and implementation of the initiative. If there are to be business unit HR professionals on the project team, you and the business unit SBP can agree on the qualifications, role, and time commitments of those HR professionals.

Piloting the initiative in business units can also reduce many problems during an enterprise-wide implementation. Pilot projects provide an opportunity to redesign some features of the solution that do not work well in the business units. The piloting can also identify where the business units need flexibility in the solution's design and usage requirements. During the planning of the initiative, use your organization's architecture model to determine what factors need to be addressed in a unique way within a specific region, facility, or function. Certainly, as a corporate SBP, you need to assist colleagues as they work to guide and influence clients within their respective areas.

SBP Tips

1. Being at the table is more of a day-to-day opportunity than a single meeting in the formal sense. Because you have gained the access, credibility, and trust to work at this level, you are helping to influence decisions that guide long-term business strategies and goals.

2. When at this level you also work to align the strategic plans of the HR function with the requirements of the business. This includes orchestrating the implementation of people initiatives in support of business plans.

3. SBPs who work at the table rarely become the expert who designs and delivers a specific solution; rather, they operate as an integrator, facilitator, and most importantly, as a business person who happens to specialize in the human side of business.

Chapter 10

Making the SBP Role Real

"You pit a good employee against a bad system, and the system will win almost every time."

Geary Rummler

If the SBP role is real, Strategic Business Partners will be building partnerships with business leaders, supporting strategic projects, and influencing business strategies and direction. But making this role real requires thoughtfully creating a process and a structure that allows SBPs to be successful. The SBP Example that follows demonstrates what can go wrong when thoughtful planning does not occur. In this chapter, we will share our experiences regarding how to plan for and make the SBP role real.

SBP Example

Good Intentions with Ineffective Execution Yields Limited Results

In our consulting practice, we began work with an HR function after the group had attempted to transition into a more strategic and business-linked department. They determined that all HR Generalists would become Business Partners and assigned these individuals to specific functions and groups within the organization. Each of the eight Business Partners was tasked to grow strong business-linked partnerships with key leaders in the functions supported, and through these partnerships, identify opportunities for strategic work. A skill-building workshop provided these eight individuals with the capability to fill their new role. Unfortunately, HR management had given little thought to how the transactional and tactical work currently managed by these individuals was to be completed. As a result, that type of work continued to flow in, limiting time available to work in the new role of Business Partner. And, because these individuals were so busy, they were not motivated to seek opportunities in which to partner at a strategic level. Why seek more work when they were already challenged to do what was on their desk each day? If they were successful in obtaining a strategic project, they had little confidence they could support the project effectively. Six months into the change process, little had changed other than the job titles for these eight people.

We have worked with numerous HR functions as they design and implement a transition plan for moving into a more strategic role. In our consultations, we borrow heavily from the work of Geary Rummler and Alan Brache in their book, *Improving Performance: How to Manage the White Space on the Organization*

Chart (1995). In essence, we guide HR departments to make decisions regarding four architectural elements in their function: mission, process, structure, and people.

Crafting a Mission for a Strategic HR Function

A mission statement indicates the reason why a department or organization exists. It needs to be short, concise, and easily communicated to others, particularly those who are working in support of it. It is also important that the mission statement for an HR function, designed to be strategic, is results-focused and not solution-focused. Compare these two mission statements from different HR departments:

- *Traditional HR Mission:* To ensure capable people are in the right jobs at the right time.
- *Strategic HR Mission:* To implement strategies and initiatives which align and strengthen the organization, resulting in enhanced employee performance and improved business results.

The traditional mission focuses on *capable* people being in the right jobs at the right time, while the strategic mission focuses on the results to be derived from HR implementing strategies and initiatives. These results include enhancement of employee *performance* and improved business results. The strategies and initiatives are a means to an end, and not the end.

It is important that the mission statement support the characteristics of a strategic HR function. You want everyone within Human Resources to see and appreciate how this strategic HR function is different from how things worked in the past. There are eight characteristics that separate a traditional HR function from a strategic one; they are displayed in Table 10.1.

Table 10.1 Characteristics of Traditional and Strategic HR Functions

TRADITIONAL HR APPROACH	*STRATEGIC HR APPROACH*

1. Results Focus

• Focus is on the solution that is implemented; the solution (i.e., training) becomes the end goal.	• Focus is on what people need to do; the solution is viewed as a means to the end of enhancing workplace performance.

*2. Reactive **and** Proactive Engagement*

• Focus is primarily on reactive entry; frequently work in a fire-fighting mode.	• Focus is on the important, not just the urgent. Work is identified both reactively and proactively. Projects are longer term in time frame and directly connect to a business goal.

3. Client-In Rather Than HR-Out

• Majority of work focuses on HR initiatives such as designing and implementing HR systems across the corporation.	• Majority of work focuses on client-initiated needs as they relate to the client's business and workplace performance requirements.

4. Solution Neutral

• Biased to a solution during initial discussions.	• Solution neutral during initial discussions.

5. Multiple Solutions

• Rely on single solutions (generally the department's specialty).	• Facilitate access to multiple solutions, both within and outside the HR department.

6. Clients and Accountabilities

• Can work independently of client partnerships. Accountability for success is segmented with HR owning quality of HR solutions and clients owning the business results.	• Partnered to a client who is active in the project (i.e., owner of the business need that is being supported). Accountability is shared; both HR and clients own accountability for performance and business results from the initiative.

TRADITIONAL   *STRATEGIC*
HR APPROACH   *HR APPROACH*

7. *Front-End Assessment*

- Front-end assessment is optional. Work environment barriers to desired performance are rarely identified.
- Front-end assessment is required. Performance gaps and causes for gaps are identified.

8. *Measurement of Solutions* **and** *Results*

- Evaluation of solutions typically occurs.
- Evaluation of solution occurs together with measurement of the performance and operational results obtained.

The arrow at the top of the table demonstrates that these characteristics are on a continuum. For example, an HR function may be characterized more strategically on Items 1, 2, and 3 while working more traditionally on the remainder of the items. The goal is to be as close to the strategic side on each of these eight characteristics as possible. Let's look at each of these characteristics in more depth.

1. *Results Focus.* Strategic HR functions are designed to focus on both the quality of solutions and the end results that occur from these solutions; traditional HR functions focus almost exclusively on the solutions. This has implications for the accountability and reward systems within the function. It is not sufficient that employees valued a training program. There must also be evidence of enhanced on-the-job performance and that the business benefited in some manner.

2. *Reactive* **and** *Proactive Engagement.* Traditional HR functions operate in a fire-fighting mode, addressing the many requests that come their way each day, many of which are transactional. In a strategic HR function, actions have been taken to offload some transactional work, so the department can on-load strategic projects. Gaining entry reactively is balanced with proactively engaging clients in projects.

3. *Client-In Rather Than HR-Out.* In a strategic function, the *majority* of work is initiated from a client's need and comes *into* the department. The work is both strategic and tactical and is client driven. In a traditional HR function, the majority of work is initiated from within the function and is implemented *out* to the organization. Examples of work that is HR-out are formation of new compensation systems, payroll systems, or performance management systems. It is not that this work is unimportant; rather, it is that strategic functions are characterized by client-driven work. An example of client-in work would be defining the best practices, standards, and work environment required for success of a position critical to a newly launched business strategy.

4. *Solution Neutral.* As we discussed throughout this book, HR professionals must maintain an objective mindset, particularly at the start of an engagement. Otherwise, there is a probability of jumping to a solution with minimal results. If HR professionals are to remain initially bias-free, then the HR function must both require and support this mindset.

5. *Multiple Solutions.* Clearly client needs can require solutions that go outside the boundaries of most HR functions. There could be a need to make capital investments in packaging equipment or to change data input and output requirements for the Information Systems Department. A strategic HR function has a legitimate role in uncovering the need for these solutions, even though another function will have primary accountability for design and implementation.

6. *Clients and Accountabilities.* This is one of the most significant differences in a truly strategic HR function. When projects are identified, there is someone from the HR function (typically the SBP) who is partnered with the client for the initiative. Together they share accountability for the *results* derived from that project. In traditional HR functions, results are siloed, with HR owning results only for the solution while the clients own the results for the business.

7. *Front-End Assessment.* One indicator of an HR function becoming more strategic is the number of performance assessment projects that are completed. At a macro level, performance assessments focus on identifying performance implications of business requirements and root causes that prevent performance from occurring. They are an integral part of the strategic HR process. Traditional front-end assessments focus on a solution, such as a training, compensation, or recruiting needs assessment.

8. *Measurement of Solutions **and** Results.* Measurement within traditional HR functions typically focuses on the quality of the solution. The most common quality measure associated with learning programs is a reaction evaluation. While strategic HR functions measure solutions, they also determine the performance and business results occurring as a result of these solutions. Not all initiatives are measured for results because not all initiatives are strategic in nature; but when strategic work is done, it is measured for impact.

Something You Can Do

Review the characteristics in Table 10.1. Compare the HR function in which you work to each of the eight sets of characteristics using the following scale.

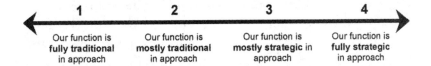

1	2	3	4
Our function is **fully traditional** in approach	Our function is **mostly traditional** in approach	Our function is **mostly strategic** in approach	Our function is **fully strategic** in approach

Which characteristics under the Traditional HR Approach most accurately describe your function? What about the characteristics under the Strategic HR Approach column? Which characteristics describe how your function works at this time? If there are other people in your department, you may want to have them complete this same type of assessment and then discuss your respective ratings. The goal is to have your entire department characterized as being close to the descriptors on the right side of the table, because these are the SHOULD characteristics for working strategically.

Use this space for your answers.

Traditional HR Characteristics of My HR Function	*Strategic HR Characteristics of My HR Function*

Aligning Process with the Strategic HR Function

Once the desired state is articulated through the mission statement, it is important to create the HR workflow processes that support the mission. Note the use of the word *processes*, in the plural form. This is because there will likely need to be several processes used; for example, what is the workflow process used to manage transactional requests? Or gain access to new clients?

Let's now look at the workflow process for identifying and managing strategic initiatives or projects. Figure 10.1 illustrates an example of this type of workflow. The process starts when you have a proactive conversation or a reframing discussion and identify a tactical or strategic need. The flow chart shows the major steps for both a strategic and a tactical project. Work that passes through the entire process provides results to both the performance of people and to the business. Let's look at each of the primary phases in this process.

Figure 10.1 HR Workflow Process for Strategic Projects

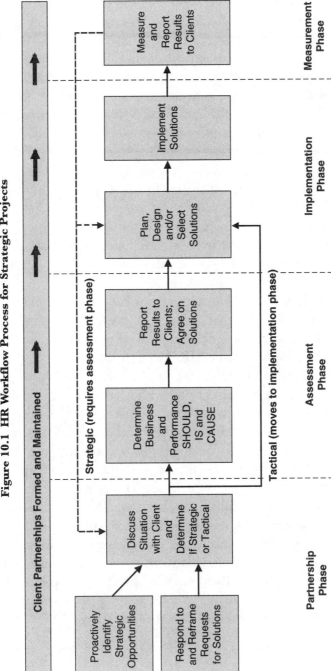

Partnership Phase involves activities associated with building and deepening relationships with clients. Of course, it also incorporates responding to requests (described in Chapter 6) and identifying strategic opportunities on which to partner proactively (Chapter 7). There are two outputs of this phase: growth of strategic client partnerships and identification of projects, both tactical and strategic, on which to work. Note that transactional requests are managed through a separate workflow process.

Assessment Phase is where you conduct one or more of the assessments described in Chapter Eight. One or more assessments are a requirement when the work is strategic in nature. When the work is tactical, you collect assessment data for the purpose of creating materials and activities for the solution to be implemented. It is vital that the HR function is resourced to either provide these assessments directly or is supported to seek the services of a supplier to do so.

In the *Implementation Phase* the various HR and learning solutions required are designed, piloted (if needed), and implemented. This phase of work has always been robust within HR functions. In a strategic HR function, there will be two ways to move into this phase. For tactical projects, you move directly to the implementation phase after agreeing with your client on the type of solution to be used; this agreement occurs in the partnership phase. For strategic work, you conduct some assessment before agreeing on solutions and moving into implementation. Regardless of entry, eventually you end up in the step that required selecting and implementing solutions.

Measurement Phase has traditionally been focused upon the least. In this phase, systemic efforts are taken to evaluate the quality of the solutions *and* the impact from the implementation of these solutions. Many strategic HR functions create their own form of a balanced scorecard so that measurement occurs in multiple areas:

- Appropriateness and effectiveness of solutions.
- Performance and business results from solutions.

- Efficiency of the process used to design and implement solutions.

- Satisfaction of clients with the HR support they received.

Across the top of the work process in Figure 10.1, you will note the words *client partnerships formed and maintained*. Developing strong partnerships is not a step in a process; rather, it is a thread of work that is woven throughout the entire process. All actions taken to support a client's need will lead to enhanced (or reduced) credibility and trust. The workflow process also shows the need to allocate resources for front-end work in strategic projects; both the partnering and assessment phases occur *before* solutions are designed and implemented.

Aligning Structure with the Strategic HR Function

Designing HR's organizational structure is appropriately done *after* the agreement on both mission and process. This approach follows the age-old truth that form follows function. Unfortunately, we find that on many occasions a new organization chart is the first step taken by HR leadership—a step that can result in the situation that we described at the beginning of this chapter. In that situation, job titles and the boxes on the HR organization chart changed, but the workflow process and work environment did not change. As a result, the HR professionals continued to do what they had always done.

When focusing on the structure needed for a strategic HR function, consider how each of the three types of work (transactional, tactical, and strategic) will be managed and what jobs within the function will be responsible for each type of work. Generally, the goals for making these decisions are to find ways to:

- Offload as much of the transactional work as possible from those who are to work strategically.

- Organize in a way to maximize efficiencies with which tactical work is completed.

- Create a structure that fully supports enlarging the portion of work that is strategic in scope.

Options for Transactional Work

As noted earlier in this book, transactional work must be completed in a quality manner. Among other risks, not to do so will reduce the credibility of the HR function to work on initiatives that are more strategic. So the question is not whether to do this work, but *how* it will be done. There are many options to consider regarding transactional work. One of the more common that we have observed is the formation of a Shared Services Center. In this model, some HR people are organized into a centralized group, becoming accountable for responding to administrative and operational requests. An example is in a large financial corporation that organized several HR Advisors into a help center. When managers or employees have a question or need, they phone this center. An HR Advisor in the help center provides the needed guidance and information. This includes responding to the many employee relations (ER) questions—requests such as "I have an employee who is not performing effectively. I could use some advice on how to manage the situation." Managing transactional work through a Shared Services Center has two benefits:

- Those responsible for doing the transactional work can be selected, developed, and rewarded for the effectiveness and efficiency with which they address the needs of those who contact the center. The HR Advisors in the financial organization who do this type of work just *love* their jobs— their enthusiasm is obvious. Moreover, this energy is in evidence to the people who utilize their services.

- Individuals in HR who are to work in the SBP role, now freed of transactional work, have more time for strategic work.

There are *other* options for managing transactional work. Technology plays a role, with the new acronym of eHR making its way into the profession. Many HR functions are investing in technology that enables employees to access and update their own records, register for a training program, and monitor their 401K account. Charles Rogers of PepsiCo indicates, "As the HR function is challenged to perform at higher levels of business partnership, it is critical to reduce the proportion of time and effort required to perform basic administrative services. Technology enables this transition," (Csoka and Hackett, 1998, p. 22).

Another option used to manage transactional work is to outsource it to others. Many organizations no longer manage their payroll or benefits administration—these are services provided by outside firms. It is reported that in 2005, 85 percent of U.S. companies will outsource at least one component of their HR functions—the number of outsourced business processes having doubled since 2000. And The Yankee Group, a Boston technology-consulting firm, is forecasting that the business processing market for domestic HR services will grow to $42 billion by 2008; worldwide the growth for the same year is placed at $80 billion (Babcock, 2004, pp. 71–72). There are now entire organizations created to manage this type of work. One example is Exult Corporation, recently acquired by Hewitt Associates for $691 million in stock. Exult went from a start-up to over 1,500 employees and 400 million dollars in revenue in its first four years of operation.

Clearly, outsourcing is a growth industry and an option that every HR function *must* consider when designing ways to provide services, particularly those of a transactional and administrative nature. One benefit, as it relates to the role of the SBP, is that transactional work is being done by others. Another benefit is the potential reduction in operational costs that can occur. While the specific reduction will vary and is dependent upon many factors including selection of the appropriate supplier, it is typical to incur a cost-per-head savings of at least 15 to 20 percent. One implication of outsourcing work is that it raises the requirement to have some HR people skillful in project and supplier management. In many HR organizations, project management is now a core competency for success.

Options for Tactical Work

The many HR solutions that are possible comprise tactical work, with examples such as compensation systems, reorganization, training and development programs, recruitment processes, organization development, and many others. These are critical services to the success of any organization—without these tactics, it would be most difficult to bring about change in how people perform. However, this type of work is also labor intensive, requiring a great deal of expertise, time, and financial investment. When HR functions transition to a more strategic approach, they must come to terms with how tactical work will be delivered. One option is to form Centers of Excellence (COEs). Similar in design to the Shared Services Centers for transactional work, a COE comprises people who are *expert* in the specific solution, such as a Rewards COE or Learning and Development COE. In this option, the COE is designed to be a resource that HR staff throughout the organization can access for support. We know of some HR functions that have even created an Assessment COE—a function organized to design, collect data from, and report findings of performance assessments and measurements. The COE is like a hub in the wheel, with the spokes being those people in HR field locations. With a COE an organization does not need to place solution experts in multiple places in the organization—they can be centralized for all to utilize. Typically, the COE is responsible for designing the solution, while HR professionals in field locations implement the solution.

As a first step in determining how to manage tactical work, we suggest that you and others in the HR function consider what services will no longer be offered directly. One HR function with which we are familiar refined the services they offered by making a decision to support solutions in only five areas. These areas included leadership development, change management, team effectiveness, talent recruitment and retention. These solution areas became the Centers of Excellence (COE) for this HR function. When a client required the services in any of these five COEs, the appropriate HR consultants would respond. If, however, a different solution was required, then the design and delivery of that solution was outsourced. The role of HR became one of managing the project rather than doing the work involved. Many learning functions have ceased delivering some categories of training, such as programs for self-development (effective writing, time management). Instead, these learning functions retain a list of qualified suppliers and refer individuals to these suppliers. Outsourcing this type of work is another option that is being utilized with increasing frequency. So, what services will your HR function no longer provide directly?

Effectively Managing Strategic Work

Actions that are taken to address the transactional and tactical work help to make room on the HR plate for strategic work. But making room is only part of the answer. HR leadership must take other actions to ensure that the transition to embrace more strategic work is sustained over time. Some suggestions we offer include the following:

- *Align with Business Units.* Identify how many SBPs are required to support the organization and align these individuals with specific business units and functions. Hold SBPs accountable for growing their knowledge of the business of the business and for forming strong partnerships with the business unit leaders. Our research indicates that one SBP can develop and maintain a business-based and *sustained* partnership with five to ten people; therefore, in mid to large organizations, an SBP can effectively support one mid-size business unit of the organization or several small ones. Larger business units and divisions may be supported by an HR team, consisting of a senior SBP (as the team leader) and some additional SBPs, HR generalists, and/or learning strategists.

- *Align with HR Process.* Ensure that each step in the strategic project workflow process has at least one HR professional assigned it. We do not mean to imply that each step in the process will have a full-time person assigned to it;

rather, there is at least one person who owns accountability for the step being performed skillfully. Lack of role clarity is one of the most common reasons for failure when transitioning to a strategic function. Therefore, early in the transition allocate time to identify what jobs are required, the number of people needed for each job, and where in the HR process each job will have accountability.

- *Reward Results.* Review the reward systems within the HR function. To what degree are rewards aligned with the type of work people will be doing? For people who concentrate on the strategic work, rewards should at least be based partially upon feedback from clients and contribution to business results. For individuals who focus on tactical work, rewards need to support the efficiency and quality with which the solutions are formed and delivered. For people who manage transactional work, rewards should take into consideration customer satisfaction and appropriateness of responses to requests.

- *Measure Results.* For measuring the function overall, we encourage the use of a balanced-scorecard approach. One of the measures might focus on the type of work that is obtained. The percentage of work generated by clients (not by HR) should increase over time so that it becomes the majority of work that is done. The percentage of work that is obtained through proactive means should also increase. Another measure could be client satisfaction with the support they are receiving from the SBPs and others. It would certainly be important to measure results from actual initiatives that are supported by HR throughout the year as well as to measure the operational efficiency with which HR services are provided.

One final comment . . . you may have found a theme in our remarks indicating that people within HR specialize in one type of work. This is a strong bias we hold, so we will label it as such. The competencies required for success in managing transactional, tactical, and strategic work are qualitatively different. Individuals who are very competent and motivated to address transactional needs generally are not as competent or as motivated in the strategic area—and the reverse is also true. Therefore, while any member of the HR team may, in the course of the year, do some of each type of work, our strong suggestion is to place people into one of the three categories of work based upon their competence and interest.

Aligning People with the Strategic HR Function

Once the structure is framed, it is time to identify specific individuals who will be placed into each of the jobs required by this structure. Obviously, in any HR function there are numerous jobs, such as recruiters, administrators, advisors, and trainers. We will only focus on the role or job of the Strategic Business Partner, as this is the focus of our work and this book.

Competencies

The first decision is to determine whether the SBP will be a role or an entire job. When it's a role, it becomes one of the hats an individual wears during the course of the year; however, there are other roles to be filled, too. The work to be accomplished is the same whether it is a role or a job; what changes is the percentage of time spent on the SBP accountabilities. The competencies required for success are also the same. Table 10.2 lists the competencies that we have found are key to the success of people who thrive and produce results when working as an SBP. The term competency is used here to reference the skills, knowledge, and attributes that an individual needs to operate effectively. While technical/process skills and knowledge of employees can be developed, you are wise to select individuals for the SBP role or job who have demonstrated at least intermediate proficiency in each of these competencies. Moreover, because attributes are very difficult to develop when they are not an innate part of the individual, it is best to hire people who already possess the required attributes.

Table 10.2 Competencies Required for Success of an SBP

TECHNICAL/PROCESS COMPETENCE

1. **ANALYSIS SKILL:** Obtaining, synthesizing, and reporting data (both narrative and quantitative).
2. **BUSINESS KNOWLEDGE**: Knowledge of how businesses function and achieve success; knowledge of these factors for the organization(s) specifically being supported.
3. **CHANGE MANAGEMENT SKILL**: Guiding others to identify and take required actions in support of a performance change initiative.
4. **FACILITATION SKILL**: Managing meetings and group processes to ensure that the objectives of the group are achieved.
5. **HR SYSTEMS AND PROCESS KNOWLEDGE**: Knowledge of multiple HR interventions and systems that can be utilized as solutions when addressing human performance needs relative to business goals.
6. **HUMAN PERFORMANCE TECHNOLOGY (HPT) UNDERSTANDING**: Knowledge of HPT as a discipline, as well as knowledge of the work of those who are its primary leaders and thinkers.
7. **INFLUENCING SKILL**: Gaining acceptance to an idea through interpersonal skills and persuasion.
8. **PROJECT MANAGEMENT SKILL**: Planning, organizing, and monitoring work done by others in support of a specific project or assignment.
9. **QUESTIONING SKILL**: Gathering information through the process of interviews and other probing methods.
10. **RELATIONSHIP-BUILDING SKILL**: Establishing and maintaining collaborative partnerships with individuals across a broad range of people and groups.
11. **STRATEGIC THINKING SKILL**: Obtaining information and identifying key issues and requirements relevant to achieving an organization's long-range goal or vision.
12. **SYSTEMIC THINKING SKILL**: Viewing the organization as a system, recognizing that the success of the whole is dependent upon the integration, understanding, and inclusion of all segments; considering the big picture.
13. **TECHNOLOGICAL SKILL**: Identifying areas in which information technology can improve employee productivity and/or customer service; selecting appropriate software solutions; utilizing HR and business software in one's own job.

ATTRIBUTES

1. **BEHAVIORAL FLEXIBILITY**: Readiness to modify approach or performance when the situation requires it.
2. **OBJECTIVITY**: Maintaining a bias-free approach to situations and people.

3. **SELF-CONFIDENCE:** Managing own performance in an effective manner when placed in new and/or challenging situations.
4. **TOLERANCE FOR AMBIGUITY:** Demonstrating comfort in situations where the goals and/or process to achieve goals are unclear and difficult to determine.

Most of the competencies in the list are self-evident. For example, someone who is to perform as an SBP and build partnerships with clients must have strong skills in building and influencing relationships. We have already discussed the criticality of HR systems and process knowledge for SBPs. The one competency that may be unfamiliar is that of Human Performance Technology (HPT) Understanding. HPT is the science of viewing organizations in a holistic and systemic manner and is based upon the works of people such as Tom Gilbert, Joe Harless, Geary Rummler, and Harold Stolovitch. Knowledge of this discipline, with an ability to draw upon its concepts and theories, is a key for success. HPT is at the foundation of the GAPS! problem-solving model described in this book.

The attribute we are most frequently asked about is Tolerance for Ambiguity. Our experience is that this is almost a make-or-break competency when it comes to successfully working as an SBP. When working strategically, there are numerous times when uncertainty reigns. Moreover, as we have mentioned with some frequency, you need to be solution neutral in the early stages of work. People who are uncomfortable with ambiguity are likely to reach agreement on solutions too quickly. Instead, you need to trust that the process and the competency of people involved will eventually result in identification of the right problem and selection of appropriate solutions. There is very little that is prescribed or procedural about your role as an SBP. There are no set lists of questions to ask or actions to take. Comfort with ambiguity is critical because many times you will be surrounded by the fog of uncertainty.

Development of SBPs

Those individuals who are selected to fill the SBP role generally require some development. The competencies we have most often observed in which new SBPs require more development include:

- Knowledge of the business.
- Questioning skills.
- Analysis skills.
- Systemic thinking skills.
- Strategic thinking skills.

There are many ways to develop people to perform successfully, only one of which is leader-led classroom experience. We have found that to have designated coaches assigned to the SBPs is a great method for developing SBP proficiency. In addition, the designated coaches can ensure that SBPs use the competencies over a sustained period of time. Effective coaches help SBPs to answer such questions as:

- How should one prepare for a reframing meeting?
- What type of assessment project should be proposed?
- How should client resistance be managed when it appears?
- What approach should be used to gain access and build partnerships with key leaders?

Sometimes the HR leader fills this coaching role. Many times, there are peers within HR who work as coaches. A key decision to make when designing a strategic HR function is who will, and how to, provide coaching and on-the-job support.

Change Tactics for a Successful Transition

There are some additional elements to consider regarding the design and implementation of a successful strategic HR function. These are tactics that will help you facilitate the change process.

1. *Strong HR Leadership Committed to Change.* As with any change, the transition to a strategic HR approach will not come without some pain. When this pain does occur, HR leaders need to demonstrate the resolve to continue the journey. Without the leader's commitment to the end goal, the transition will begin to disintegrate. What are some of the most typical pains experienced? Surprisingly, the most common can be resistance from within the function itself. We find it ironic that a profession in support of numerous organizational change initiatives can be distressed when change is occurring within its own house. We value the message of an HR leader who said to his team, "I tell people that the train has left the station and is moving to a new destination. I would like everyone on the journey, and they can influence our trip process, but the end destination is not up for vote. We *will* be working more strategically in the future."

2. *SBPs Have Direct Access to Clients.* It is not possible to support a strategic approach when those in the SBP role are precluded from working directly with their clients. If you must work through an HR colleague or if the organization's norms prevent you from working with the business leaders, the transition will be bumpy indeed!

3. *Business Unit Support for the New HR Mission.* We do not recommend a major announcement to the organization that HR has changed and people will now be working differently. However, we are supportive of HR leaders having conversations with business leaders, advising them of the change in HR's role, the drivers for this change, and how this change will benefit the organization. It is also an opportunity to respond to the business leader's questions and to articulate what actions these leaders can take to support the change.

4. *Form a Change Strategy; Monitor Progress.* Once the mission of the HR function has been formed and decisions made as to process, structure, and people, a plan for execution is developed. The transition is best managed as an *evolution*

and not a *re*volution. One approach is to have SBPs lead the way, building the partnerships and identifying opportunities to work. Others in HR continue to work as they always have. Those in the SBP role provide their clients with firsthand experience of how HR *can* work strategically. As the clients work with the SBPs and have positive results from strategic projects, the word spreads throughout the organization. One manager tells another manager. The result? An increase in the amount of client-driven work of a strategic nature. Beyond an implementation strategy and plan, it is also important to create mileposts as a way to measure progress. We have found that the transition to a strategic HR approach can take two or more years to complete. Be sure to monitor the transition toward the goal, so if a derailing is noticed, appropriate actions can be taken.

5. *Get Small Wins—and Market Them!* Nothing breeds success like success. So, early in the transition you want SBPs and others in the HR function to experience working more strategically, personally experiencing the results that can be derived. One of the best experiences is when clients invite you to do strategic work (a pull strategy). This can occur spontaneously when one client, who is satisfied with the support you provide, tells a peer-manager of the experience. As one of our clients said, "No amount of money can pay for that type of marketing—word of mouth from one manager to another." When a project has concluded with a satisfied client, it is not a time to be shy. Ask the manager to share the experience with others; you will be amazed at how strategic opportunities will begin coming your way.

6. *Communicate, Communicate, Communicate.* As with any change process, it is vital to stay connected with people within HR throughout the change process. People need to know of successes and challenges. They want to learn and grow from each other's experience. And they want

to know how the transition is progressing from both their own and the clients' perspectives. Staff meetings provide an opportunity for people to share experiences; so does a chat room or bulletin board to be accessed by people in the HR function. Design communication to occur in all directions: from the HR leaders to employees, from one SBP to other SBPs, between clients and people within the HR function. The basic plan should be to celebrate successes and learn from experiences that were not so successful.

Something You Can Do

Now that you have read much or all of the book, we want to give you an opportunity to examine the readiness of you and your organization to transition to a strategic HR approach. The following is a self-assessment instrument to assist you in determining readiness to move forward with the transition to an SBP role.

Section One: Identifies competencies required of Strategic Business Partners. Assess your current skill level with each of these competencies.

Section Two: Identifies what Strategic Business Partners must do on the job to fulfill their accountabilities. Assess your current level of skill to perform each of these requirements.

Section Three: Identifies organizational factors that, when in place, support Strategic Business Partners and the work they do. When these factors are absent, they are barriers to success. Assess your current HR function and its readiness to support the work of Strategic Business Partners.

Section One: Competencies and Attributes

The following competencies have been identified as those required to be successful Strategic Business Partners. This list is divided into two categories:

- *Technical/Process Competence.* Those where your skill and knowledge can be developed.

- *Attributes.* These are characteristics or traits and, therefore, are difficult to develop.

By placing a checkmark in the appropriate column, rate your level of competence for each item on this page. Use the rating key at the end of this section as a guide for your ratings. Then list your strengths and developmental needs in the table at the end of this exercise.

TECHNICAL/PROCESS COMPETENCIES	*Level of Competence*		
	Proficient	*Adequate*	*Basic*
1. **ANALYSIS SKILL**: Obtain, synthesize, and report data (both narrative and quantitative).			
2. **BUSINESS KNOWLEDGE**: Knowledge of how businesses function and achieve success; knowledge of these factors for the organization(s) specifically being supported.			
3. **CHANGE MANAGEMENT SKILL**: Guide others to identify and take required actions in support of a performance change initiative.			

	Level of Competence		
TECHNICAL/PROCESS COMPETENCIES	*Proficient*	*Adequate*	*Basic*
4. **FACILITATION SKILL**: Manage meetings and group processes to ensure that the objectives of the group are achieved.			
5. **HR SYSTEMS AND PROCESS KNOWLEDGE**: Knowledge of multiple HR interventions and systems that can be utilized as solutions when addressing human performance needs relative to business goals.			
6. **HUMAN PERFORMANCE TECHNOLOGY (HPT) UNDERSTANDING**: Knowledge of HPT as a discipline, as well as knowledge of the work of those who are its primary leaders and thinkers.			
7. **INFLUENCING SKILL**: Gain acceptance of an idea through interpersonal skills and persuasion.			
8. **PROJECT MANAGEMENT SKILL**: Plan, organize, and monitor work done by others in support of a specific project or assignment.			
9. **QUESTIONING SKILL**: Gather information through the process of interviews and other probing methods.			
10. **RELATIONSHIP-BUILDING SKILL**: Establish and maintain collaborative partnerships with individuals across a broad range of people and groups.			
11. **STRATEGIC THINKING SKILL**: Obtain information and identify key issues and requirements relevant to achieving an organization's long-range goal or vision.			
12. **SYSTEMIC THINKING SKILL**: View the organization as a system, recognizing that the success of the whole is dependent upon the integration, understanding, and inclusion of all segments; consider the big picture.			

	Level of Competence		
TECHNICAL/PROCESS COMPETENCE	Proficient	Adequate	Basic
13. **TECHNOLOGICAL SKILL**: Identify areas in which information technology can improve employee productivity and/or customer service; select appropriate software solutions; utilize HR and business software in one's own job.			
ATTRIBUTES			
14. **BEHAVIORAL FELXIBILTY**: Readiness to modify approach or performance when the situation requires it.			
15. **OBJECTIVITY**: Maintain a bias-free approach to situations and people.			
16. **SELF-CONFIDENCE**: Manage own performance in an effective manner when placed in new and/or challenging situations.			
17. **TOLERANCE FOR AMBIGUITY**: Demonstrate comfort in situations where the goals and/or process to achieve goals are unclear and difficult to determine.			

Rating Key: *PROFICIENT* = I consistently demonstrate skill while managing routine, unique and difficult situations.
ADEQUATE = I demonstrate skill in routine situations, but require coaching on how to apply the competency in unique and/or difficult situations.
BASIC = I have only foundation skills in this area.

Section Two: Strategic Business Partner Accountabilities

The SBP accountabilities are listed in this section. Using the rating key at the end of this section, rate your skill level for each of these accountabilities by placing a checkmark in the appropriate column. Then indicate

your areas of proficiency, as well as for development, in
the table at the close of this exercise.

ACCOUNTABILITIES		*Current Skill Level*		
BUILD CLIENT PARTNERSHIPS	*Proficient*	*Adequate*	*Basic*	*Not Applicable*
18. Gain face time and access with my sustained clients.				
19. Build credibility with my client(s).				
20. Develop trust with my client(s).				
IDENTIFY AND PARTNER TO SUPPORT STRATEGIC PROJECTS				
21. Reframe requests for solutions to identify strategic opportunities.				
22. Manage proactive conversations with clients to identify strategic opportunities on which to work.				
23. Use appropriate assessment techniques when supporting a strategic project.				
24. Select and implement effective solutions.				
INFLUENCE BUSINESS STRATEGIES AND DIRECTION				
25. Contribute to the formation of business strategies and plans.				
26. Integrate the HR strategic plan and initiatives into the business plan.				
27. Implement people initiatives in support of the business plan.				

Rating Key: *PROFICIENT* = I consistently demonstrate skill in performing this accountability in routine, unique and difficult situations.
ADEQUATE = I demonstrate skill in performing this accountability in routine situations, but require coaching when in a unique and/or difficult situations.
BASIC = I demonstrate only foundation skills in performing this accountability.
NOT APPLICABLE = I have had no opportunity to do this, so I cannot assess current skill.

Section Three: HR Organization Factors

This is a partial list of factors within your HR organization that can affect your transition to being an effective SBP. Using the rating key at the end of this section, indicate with a checkmark how each factor impacts upon your effectiveness as an SBP.

HR ORGANIZATION FACTORS	This Factor Supports Me	This Factor Neither Supports Nor Challenges Me	This Factor Challenges Me
28. An HR workflow process has been formed for identifying and completing strategic projects.			
29. The HR workflow process for strategic projects has been communicated to and is understood by those who support the process.			
30. My transactional work is being reduced through outsourcing, use of vendors, or other means.			
31. Support for tactical work is available from Centers of Excellence or other resources.			

32. As an SBP I have been assigned to support specific business units, functions, and/or the enterprise itself.			
33. Specific HR professionals are responsible for specific steps in the HR workflow process for strategic projects; respective roles are clear.			
34. For strategic work, I am rewarded based upon the feedback from my clients and my contribution to business results.			
35. I receive coaching in those competencies and activities where I need development.			

Rating Key: *THIS FACTOR SUPPORTS ME* = The factor is present, and I find it supportive of my work as an SBP.
THIS FACTOR NEITHER SUPPORTS NOR CHALLENGES ME = Whether the factor is or is not present, I find it having minimal impact upon me as an SBP.
THIS FACTOR CHALLENGES ME = The factor is not present and that is a problem for my work as an SBP.

Use this space for your answers to the assessment.

Competencies and Attributes Where I am Proficient	*Competencies and Attributes Where I Need Development*

SBP Accountabilities Where I am Proficient	SBP Accountabilities Where I Need Development
HR Organizational Factors That Support Me	HR Organizational Factors That Challenge Me

Once you have completed the exercise, review your responses in the table. Where are the strengths and enhancers to moving forward as an SBP? What are the primary barriers or challenges you face? Now consider how you can take advantage of your strengths and the enhancers to move forward as an SBP. Also consider what actions you can take to either remove the barriers or influence others to do so. List options for you to develop additional skill in competencies where needed. Note your thoughts in the box on the following page.

Actions I can take to support an effective transition to a strategic HR approach.
Actions I can take to influence others to take to support an effective transition to a strategic HR approach.

SBP Tips

1. For the Strategic Business Partner role to become real, the function itself must be strategic in how it operates. There are eight factors (described in this chapter) that you can use to determine whether your HR function does operate in a strategic manner.

2. To successfully transition to a strategic HR function, you need to create a workflow process that describes the steps an SBP takes to:

   - Identify strategic projects.
   - Use appropriate assessment techniques.
   - Select and implement effective solutions.
   - Measure the quality of the solutions and their impact upon results.

3. To be effective as an SBP, you need to develop skills and knowledge in thirteen competencies that are critical for success. There are also four attributes (your traits or characteristics) that are critical to success as an SBP. Strength in these four attributes will greatly increase your probability for success as an SBP.

4. The transition to a strategic HR function has many potential roadblocks. To make the transition successfully, complete an objective assessment of the current HR situation in your organization and develop a transition plan. Then work the plan.

5. It is not a matter of *if* Human Resource functions will become strategic. It is *when and how* that transition will take place.

Some Closing Thoughts

We are reminded of the old adage that when the tide comes in, all boats will rise. The tide coming in for HR is that of opportunity and organizational need. As noted in our Introduction, opportunity is knocking at HR's door. Our business leaders need and want to optimize the talents of their people. And focusing on the people side of business is the reason HR exists. The opportunity is here and now for HR to be working strategically and to be at the table. When an HR function successfully moves into this role, all of HR and the entire organization benefit. The credibility of HR that many in the profession feel is lacking will be evident; the vision of truly making a difference in the organization will be realized.

We hope you have found some useful tips and guidance in this book for making the SBP role real within your organization. We also hope you are inspired to move in this direction. For us, it is not a matter of *if*, but of *how* this movement in HR will occur. Actually, the movement is underway and will be well placed in many organizations in a few years. We concur with David Ulrich when he said, "the future of HR is phenomenal," (Bates, p. 32).

We'd Like to Hear from You

Our professional interest continues to focus on assisting people in the HR field to link closely with the businesses they support, making a difference in the work they do. We continually advance our knowledge of practices that work (as well as those that don't!) by communicating with people who are practicing a strategic HR approach. What are you learning from your personal experiences as an SBP or as someone who leads people who work in this role? What practices have you found effective? Are you doing anything different after reading this book? We welcome your feedback. Please e-mail your comments to us at mail@partners-in-change.com. May your experiences as a Strategic Business Partner bring you, and your organization, much success!

Tools

GAPS! Map

Business Need: _____   Employee Group: _____

G

Go
for
the
SHOULD

Business SHOULD	Performance SHOULD

A

Analyze
the
IS

Business IS	Performance IS

P

Pin Down
the
CAUSES

Factors External to Organization	Factors Internal to Organization (Work Environment Needs)	Factors Internal to Individuals (Capability Needs)

Outside the   Within the
Business Unit   Business Unit

S

Select
the Right
SOLUTIONS

© 2002, 2005 Partners in Change, Inc.

REFRAMING REQUESTS

Interview Format for a Reframing Discussion

---

1. Confirm and agree on purpose(s) for the meeting.

   a. Reference previous discussions.

   b. State your purposes for meeting.

   c. Seek client's purposes for meeting.

   d. Confirm time available for meeting.

2. Confirm personal understanding of the situation.

   a. Summarize what you know.

   b. Verify desired result(s) client seeks from the project.

3. Ask questions beginning with the highest-level need presented.

Suggestion: Write questions in the order in which you will be asking them. Leave space for note-taking purposes. Consider this a starter set of questions and not a complete list of questions.

Note: Items 4 through 6 cannot be prepared in advance; these are items discussed in the reframing meeting as it is concluding.

4. Summarize what is known/unknown about the situation.

   a. Indicate what is known about the situation.

   b. Indicate what is unknown.

   c. Discuss areas where more information is needed and the benefits for obtaining this information.

     d. Determine whether situation qualifies as a strategic performance improvement project using the following criteria:

       _____ Direct access to true client.

       _____ A business need exists.

       _____ Client seeks performance change or improvement.

       _____ Client willing to share accountability for producing change.

       _____ Client will provide time and access to people to conduct required assessment.

       _____ Situation focuses on a group of people.

5. Select *one* of the following as the plan to use.

     a. Agree in principle to obtain more information (if qualifies as strategic work) and indicate a date when you will return with a proposal.

     b. Form the action plan now for obtaining information that is currently unknown (if qualifies as strategic work).

     c. Respond to client's request, acknowledging limitations (if qualifies as tactical work).

6. Agree on next steps for you and for the client.

PROACTIVE INTERVIEW GUIDE

DEMOGRAPHIC INFORMATION

NAME OF CLIENT: _____

POSITION:_____

BUSINESS UNIT/FUNCTION: _____

INTERVIEW DATE: _____ INTERVIEW TIME: ____

PROFILE OF BUSINESS UNIT/FUNCTION

NOTE TO CONSULTANT: To the degree possible, obtain the following information prior to the conversation. At the beginning of the discussion, affirm the information as appropriate. If the information was not obtained prior to the discussion, obtain it from the manager before beginning with the formal interview process.

- Organization Chart for Business Unit/Function
- Business Plan
- Demographic Information on Employees
    - Number of employees for each employee job and group
    - Geographical location(s) of employees
- Products and Services Produced by Business Unit/Function
- Customers and Competitors of the Business Unit/Function
- Alliances, Joint Ventures, and/or Acquisitions Involving the Business Unit/Function
- Operational Metrics Typically Used to Measure the Operational Health of the Business Unit/Function
- Other Items of Relevance/Recent News Regarding the Client/Business Unit/Function

INTRODUCTORY COMMENTS

1. Introductions.

2. Overview purposes for conversation.
   NOTE: *These are examples of the opening remarks that can be made.*

   - Our organization's rapidly changing business environment is requiring a heightened focus on employee and managerial performance.

   - I and my department are committed to supporting our customer organizations by ensuring that the actions we take are tightly linked to the business needs of those organizations.

   - One way we work is to respond to requests for assistance that are brought to our attention. Generally, these requests come because there is a problem to be resolved.

   - Another way we want to work more frequently is to identify partnering opportunities in a proactive manner. This means working together to *anticipate* needs rather than waiting until there is a problem.

   - The conversation we are about to have is designed for this purpose. At minimum, I will be learning more about your current and future business requirements. This knowledge about your business will promote my effectiveness in working with you and others in this department.

   - However, it is also possible that we will collectively identify an area where partnering together in support of a business need you have would be beneficial. In this way, we are *anticipating* the needs you have rather than reacting to them.

PROACTIVE INTERVIEW GUIDE

INTRODUCTORY COMMENTS
(continued)

3. Explain agenda for conversation:
   - In this conversation, I will be asking questions about the business initiatives and goals that are critical for your business unit/function. It would be helpful to discuss the forces and factors that may be challenging accomplishment of these goals as well as the performance requirements for people in your organization if these goals are to be achieved.
   - It is possible that we might determine an opportunity neither of us was thinking of, where support from me and my department would be a value-add to you. If that is the case, we will move ahead with that discussion.
   - Do you have any questions before we begin?
4. Affirm amount of time available for the conversation.

CURRENT BUSINESS GOALS

I would like to begin our conversation by identifying one major business goal or initiative for (*name of business unit/function*) in the next twelve months. By business goal I mean a specific objective you have that is, ideally, measured in operational terms.

GOAL 1: _____
_____

1. Why is this an important goal at this time? What are the driving forces behind this goal?

2. a) What indicators will be used to measure this goal and what are the actuals now? b) What should the measures be at the end of the year?

3. What strategies are being used to accomplish this goal?

4. What forces or factors outside the organization are going to challenge the achievement of this goal?

5. What about inside the organization—are there any factors that will challenge achievement of this goal?

EMPLOYEE GROUPS

6. Within your business unit/function, which employee group(s) will most directly contribute to the achievement of this goal through their performance?

    NOTE: *Discuss each employee group separately and ask the questions that follow.*

Employee Group: _____

7. Considering the business goal and challenges that you are facing, what must people in this group do more, better, or differently if they are to successfully support this goal?

8. What are the major gaps between what you need people to be doing on-the-job to support this business goal and what people are typically doing now?

9. What barriers, if any, will challenge people performing as required?

10. **Situational Question:** *Ask the following question if there were "I don't know" responses and/or vague responses.*

Would it be of benefit to obtain more information regarding:

_____ What people in this group need to do differently if this goal is to be achieved?

_____ What gaps exist between required and current performance of people?

_____ What barriers exist that challenge people from performing as you need?

CLOSE

1. SUMMARIZE key learnings from the conversation regarding:

   • Business Goals.

   • Performance Requirements.

2. SUMMARIZE next steps that can include any/all of the following:

   a. If there are any project(s) that have been identified as potential areas to work on:

   ✓ Indicate that it would be helpful to have a follow-up conversation to discuss the situation(s) in depth.

   ✓ Establish a date for that conversation to occur.

   b. Learning more about the manager's business unit/function:

   ✓ Indicate your interest in learning more about the business of the business within this manager's span of control.

   ✓ ASK: *What suggestion do you have as to what I could read, or people with whom I might meet, to deepen my knowledge of this business unit/fuunction?*

   c. Explaining your role:

   ✓ ASK: *Are there any questions you have about my role or our department and our work that I might answer at this time?*

   d. Continued conversations:

   ✓ Indicate interest in maintaining communication with this manager.

   ✓ ASK: *Would it be possible for me to call in the next _____ months to set up another time when we might meet to learn of any new or different needs you may have at that time?*

3. THANK INDIVIDUAL for his/her time. Affirm next steps (if any) to be taken.

WORKSHEET FOR RATING POSSIBLE SOLUTIONS

Root Cause (or symptom)	Possible Solution (or needed information)	Ratings (0 to 3)*					Decision
		A	E	F	OA	IEA	

*Ratings: 0=Unacceptable   A = Appropriateness   OA = Organizational Acceptability
             1=Low   E = Economics   IEA = Individual Employee Acceptability
             2=Acceptable   F = Feasibility
             3=Exceptional

References

Preface

Cheese, P., Brakeley, H., and Clinton, D. "The High-Performance Workforce Study: 2002/2003," Accenture. Retrieved from www.accenture.com in June 2004.

Lawler, E. E. III, and Mohrman, S. A. "HR as a Strategic Partner: What Does It Take to Make It Happen?" Center for Effective Organizations, Marshall School of Business, University of Southern California, January 2003.

Introduction: From Value Sapping to Value Adding

Bates, Steve. "Facing the Future." *HR Magazine*. SHRM, July 2002, pp. 26–32.

Canadian HR Reporter, "Link between HR Execs and Bottom Line." HRReporter.com, February 2003. http://www.hrreporter.com/loginarea/members/viewing.asp?articleno=1682.

Caudron, Shari. "HR is Dead . . . Long Live HR." *Workforce,* January 2003, pp. 26–30.

Esen, Even and SHRM. "Human Resource Outsourcing Report." SHRM Research. July 2004.

Stewart, Thomas. "Taking on the Last Bureaucracy." *Fortune,* January 15, 1996, p. 15.

Stolz, Richard. "Ah, To Be Strategic." *Workindex.com,* January 20, 2004, pp. 20–32.

Ulrich, David. "A New Mandate for Human Resources." *Harvard Business Review,* January-February 1998, pp. 124–134.

Chapter 1: Key Concepts for Partnering Strategically

Rummler, G. A., and Brache, A. P. *Improving Performance: How to Manage the White Space on the Organization Chart.* San Francisco: Jossey-Bass Publishers, 1995.

Chapter 2: The SBP Model

Lawler, E. E. III, and Mohrman, S. A. "HR as a Strategic Partner: What does it take to make it happen?" Center for Effective Organizations, Marshall School of Business, University of Southern California, January 2003.

Chapter 4: Gaining Credibility and Trust

Lawler, E. E. III, and Mohrman, S. A. "Creating a Strategic Human Resources Organization: An Assessment of Trends and New Directions." Stanford University Press, Stanford, CA, 2003.

Lawler, E.E. III, and Mohrman, S. A. "HR as a Strategic Partner: What Does it Take to Make it Happen?" Center for Effective Organizations, Marshall School of Business, University of Southern California, 2003.

Steinburg, C. "Partnerships and the Line." *Training & Development,* October 1991, pp. 28–35.

Ulrich, D., and Beatty, D. "From Players to Partners: Extending the HR Playing Field." *Human Resource Management,* Volume 1, Issue 4, 2001, pp. 293–307.

Chapter 7: Proactively Identify Strategic Opportunities

Conner, D. *Leading at the Edge of Chaos: How to Create The Nimble Organization.* New York: John Wiley & Sons Inc., 1998.

Chapter 8: When the Client Says "Yes"

Stolovitch, H., and Keeps, E. "Implementation Phase: Performance Improvement Interventions," in the book *Moving from Training to Performance: A Practical Guidebook.* ASTD and Berrett-Koehler Publishers, Inc., 1998, p. 113.

Chapter 9: Being At the Table

Adkins, Sam S. "Beneath the Tip of the Iceberg." *Training and Development.* ASTD, February 2004, pp. 28-33.
Bossidy, L., and Charan, R. *The Discipline of Getting Things Done.* New York: Crown Business, 2002.
Brockbank, Wayne. "HR's Future on the Way to a Presence." *Human Resource Management,* Spring 1997, Volume 36, Number 1, pp. 65–69.
Lawler, E. E. III, and Mohrman, S. A. "HR as a Strategic Partner: What Does It Take to Make It Happen?" Center for Effective Organizations, Marshall School of Business, University of Southern California, January 2003.

Chapter 10: Making the SBP Role Real

Babcock, Pamela. "Slicing Off Pieces of HR." HR Outsourcing Special Report, *HR Magazine,* July 2004, pp. 71–76.
Bates, Steve. "Facing the Future." *HR Magazine.* SHRM, July 2002, pp. 26–32.

Csoka, Louis S., and Hackett, Brian. "Transforming the HR Function for Global Business Success: A Research Report." The Conference Board, New York, 1998.

Rummler, G. A., and Brache, A. P. *Improving Performance: How to Manage the White Space on the Organization Chart.* San Francisco: Jossey-Bass Publishers, 1995.

Resource List

BOOKS

Assessment

Barksdale, S., and Lund, T. *Rapid Needs Analysis: Tools, Worksheets, and Job Aids to Help You Determine in "Internet Time" If Analysis is Needed, Find and Analyze a Performance Problem Fast, Recommend the Best Solution to Meet Business Needs.* Alexandria, VA: ASTD, 2001.

Cooper, K. C. *Effective Competency Modeling and Reporting: A Step-by-Step Guide for Improving Individual and Organizational Performance.* New York: American Management Association, 2000.

Phillips, J. J. (ed.). *In Action: Performance Analysis and Consulting.* Alexandria, VA: ASTD, 2000.

Robinson, D. G., and Robinson, J. C. *Training for Impact: How to Link Training to Business Needs and Measure the Results.* San Francisco: Jossey-Bass Publishers, 1989.

Rogers, R. E., and Fong, J. Y. *Organizational Assessment: Diagnosis and Intervention*. Amherst, MA: Human Resource Development Press, 2000.

Rossett, A. *First Things Fast: A Handbook for Performance Analysis*. San Francisco: Pfeiffer, 1998.

Sanghi, S. *The Handbook of Competency Mapping: Understanding, Designing and Implementing Competency Models in Organizations*. London, UK: Sage Publications Ltd., 2004.

Stolovitch, H. D., and Keeps, E. J. *Front-End Analysis and Return on Investment Toolkit*. San Francisco: Pfeiffer, 2004.

Zwell, M. *Creating a Culture of Competence*. New York: John Wiley & Sons, Inc., 2000.

Measurement

Anderson, M. *Bottom-Line Organizational Development: Implementing & Evaluating Strategic Change for Lasting Value*. Burlington, MA: Butterworth-Heinemann, 2003.

Becker, B. E., Huselid, M. A., and Ulrich, D. *The HR Scorecard: Linking People, Strategy, and Performance*. Boston: Harvard Business School Press, 2001.

Brinkerhoff, R. O. *The Success Case Method: Find Out Quickly What's Working and What's Not*. San Francisco: Berrett-Koehler Publishers, 2003.

Combs, W. L., and Falletta, S. V. *The Targeted Evaluation Process: A Performance Consultant's Guide to Asking the Right Questions and Getting the Results*. Alexandria, VA: ASTD, 2000.

Fitz-Enz, J. *The ROI of Human Capital: Measuring the Economic Value of Employee Performance*. New York: American Management Association, 2000.

Fitz-Enz, J., and Davison, B. *How to Measure Human Resource Management* (3rd ed.). New York: American Management Association, 2001.

Hale, J. *Performance Based Evaluation: Tools and Techniques to Measure the Impact of Training*. San Francisco: Jossey Bass/Pfeiffer, 2002.

Kirkpatrick, D. L. *Evaluating Training Programs: The Four Levels* (2nd ed.). San Francisco: Berrett-Koehler Publishers, 1998.

Pfau, B. N., and Kay, I. T. *The Human Capital Edge: 21 People Management Practices Your Company Must Implement (or Avoid) to Maximize Shareholder Value.* New York: McGraw-Hill Trade, 2001.

Phillips, J. J. *Return on Investment in Training and Performance Improvement Programs* (2nd ed.). Houston: Gulf Publishing Company, 2003.

Phillips, J. J., and Stone, R. *How to Measure Training Results: A Practical Guide to Tracking the Six Key Indicators.* New York: McGraw-Hill Trade, 2002.

Phillips, J. J., Stone, R. D., and Phillips, P.P. *The Human Resources Scorecard.* Houston: Gulf Publishing Company, 2001.

Phillips, P. P. *The Bottomline on ROI: Basics, Benefits, & Barriers to Measuring Training & Performance Improvement.* Atlanta: CEP Press, 2002.

Phillips, P. P., and Phillips, J. J. (eds.). In *Action: Measuring Return on Investment, Volume 3.* Alexandria, VA: ASTD, 2001.

Russ-Eft, D., and Preskill, H. *Evaluation in Organizations: A Systematic Approach to Enhancing Learning, Performance, and Change.* New York: Perseus Publishing, 2001.

Ulrich, D., Goldsmith, M., Carter, L., Bolt, J., and Smallwood, N. *The Change Champion's Fieldguide: Strategies and Tools for Leading Change in Your Organization.* Waltham, MA: Best Practice Publications, LLC, 2003.

Organizational Architecture Models

Ackoff, R. L. *Re-Creating the Corporation: A Design of Organizations for the 21st Century.* New York: Oxford University Press, 1999.

Brickley, J. A., Smith, C. W., and Zimmerman, J. L. *Managerial Economics and Organizational Architecture.* New York: McGraw-Hill, 2003.

Carter, L., Goldsmith, M., and Giber, D. J. *Best Practices in Organization Development and Change: Culture, Leadership, Retention, Performance, and Coaching.* New York: John Wiley & Sons, 2001.

Fitzgerald, S. P. *Organizational Models.* New York: John Wiley & Sons, 2002.

Galbraith, J. R. *Designing Organizations: An Executive Guide to Strategy, Structure, and Process.* New York: John Wiley & Sons, 2001.

Galbraith, J. R., Downey, D., and Kates, A. *Designing Dynamic Organizations: A Hands-on Guide for Leaders at All Levels.* New York: American Management Association, 2001.

Morabito, J., Sack, I. and Bhate, A. *Organization Modeling: Innovative Architectures for the 21st Century.* New York: Prentice-Hall, 1999.

Nadler, D., Tushman, M., and Nadler, M. B. *Competing by Design: The Power of Organizational Architecture.* New York: Oxford University Press, 1997.

Rigsby, J. A., and Greco, G. *Mastering Strategy: Insights from the World's Greatest Leaders and Thinkers.* New York: McGraw-Hill Companies, 2002.

Rummler, G. A., and Brache, A. P. *Improving Performance: How to Manage the White Space on the Organization Chart.* San Francisco: Jossey-Bass, 1995.

Strategic HR Functions

Effron, M., Gandossy, R., and Goldsmith, M. *Human Resources in the 21st Century.* New York: John Wiley & Sons, 2003.

Enabling Human Resources as a Strategic Partner. Houston, TX: American Productivity & Quality Center, 2000.

Gilley, A. M., Bierema, L. L., and Callahan, J. *Critical Issues in HRD: A New Agenda for the Twenty-First Century.* New York: Perseus Publishing, 2002.

Gilley, J. W., and Gilley, A. M. *Strategically Integrated HRD: A Six-Step Approach to Creating Results-Driven Programs Performance.* New York: Perseus Books Group, 2002.

Gilley, J. W., and Maycunich, A. *Organizational Learning, Performance, and Change: An Introduction to Strategic Human Resource Development.* New York: Perseus Books Group, 2000.

Grundy, T., and Brown, L. *Value-based Human Resource Strategy: Developing Your HR Consultancy Role.* Burlington, MA: Butterworth-Heinemann, 2003.

Holbeche, L. *Aligning Human Resources and Business Strategy.* Burlington, MA: Butterworth-Heinemann, 2001.

LaBonte, T. J. *Building a New Performance Vision: Break Down Organizational Silos and Create a Unified Approach to Human Performance Improvement.* Alexandria, VA: ASTD, 2001.

Lastimado, B. *Increasing Your Human Resources Profession's Value: Make Them Want You for a Strategic Partner.* Lanham, MD: University Press of America, 2003.

Lawler, E. E. III, and Mohrman, S. A. *Creating an Effective Human Resources Organization: Trends and New Directions.* Palo Alto, CA: Stanford University Press, 2003.

Lawler, Edward E., Ulrich, David, Fitz-enz, Jac, Madden, James and Maruca, Regina. *Human Resources Business Process Outsourcing: Transforming How HR Gets Its Work Done.* San Francisco: Jossey-Bass, 2004.

Mello, J. A. *Strategic Human Resource Management.* Mason, OH: South-Western Thomas Learning, 2001.

Sartain, L., and Finney, M. *HR from the Heart: Inspiring Stories and Strategies for Building the People Side of Great Business.* New York: American Management Association, 2003.

Ulrich, D. *Delivering Results: A New Mandate for Human Resource Professionals.* Boston: Harvard Business School Press, 1998.

Ulrich, D. *Human Resources Champions.* Boston: Harvard Business School Press, 1997.

Ulrich, D., Losey, M. R., and Lake, G. (eds.) *Tomorrow's HR Management: 48 Thought Leaders Call for Change.* New York: John Wiley & Sons, 1997.

Weiss, D. S. *High Performance HR: Leveraging Human Resources for Competitive Advantage.* New York: John Wiley & Sons, 2000.

Human Performance Technology

Brinkerhoff, R. O., and Apking, A. M. *High Impact Learning.* New York: Perseus Books Group, 2001.

Chevalier, R. *Human Performance Technology Revisited.* Silver Spring, MD: ISPI, 2004.

Clark, R. E., and Estes, F. *Turning Research into Results: A Guide to Selecting the Right Performance Solutions.* Atlanta: CEP Press, 2002.

Gilbert, T. F. *Human Competence: Engineering Worthy Performance* (ISPI Tribute Edition). Silver Spring, MD and Amherst, MA: ISPI/HRD Press, 1996.

Piskurich, G. M. (ed.). *HPI Essentials: A Just-the-Facts, Bottom-Line Primer on Human Performance Improvement.* Alexandria, VA: ASTD, 2002.

Rothwell, W. J., Hohne, C. K., and King, S. B. *Human Performance Improvement: Building Practitioner Competence.* Houston: Gulf Publishing Company, 2000.

Rummler, G. A., and Brache, A. P. *Improving Performance: How to Manage the White Space on the Organization Chart.* San Francisco: Jossey-Bass, 1995.

Sanders, E. S., and Thiagarajan, S. *Performance Intervention Maps: 36 Strategies for Solving Your Organization's Problems.* Alexandria, VA: ASTD, 2001.

Stolovitch, H. D., and Keeps, E. J. *Training Ain't Performance.* Silver Spring, MD: ISPI, 2004.

Stolovitch, H. D., and Keeps, E. J. (eds.) *Handbook of Human Performance Technology: Improving Individual and Organizational Performance Worldwide* (2nd ed.). San Francisco: Jossey-Bass/Pfeiffer, 1999.

Van Tiem, D. M., Moseley, J. L, and Dessinger, J. C. *Fundamentals of Performance Technology: A Guide to Improving People, Process, and Performance* (2nd ed.). Silver Spring, MD: ISPI, 2000.

Willmore, Joe. *Performance Basics.* Washington, DC. ASTD Press, 2004. San Francisco: Jossey Bass Business and Management Series, 2004.

Consulting and Strategic HR Partnering

Bellman, G. M. *The Consultant's Calling: Bringing Who You Are to What You Do (rev. ed.).* San Francisco: Jossey-Bass, 2001.

Bellman, G. M. *Getting Things Done When You Are Not in Charge: How to Succeed from a Support Position* (2nd ed.). San Francisco: Berrett-Koehler Publishers, 2001.

Blanchard, K., Robinson, D., and Robinson, J. *Zap the Gaps: Target Higher Performance and Achieve It!* New York: HarperCollins Publishers, 2002.

Block, P. *The Answer to How Is Yes: Acting on What Matters.* San Francisco: Berrett-Koehler Publishers, 2003.

Block, P. *Flawless Consulting: A Guide to Getting Your Expertise Used* (2nd ed.). San Francisco: Jossey Bass/Pfeiffer, 2000.

Block, P. *The Flawless Consulting Fieldbook and Companion: A Guide to Understanding Your Expertise.* San Francisco: Pfeiffer, 2000.

Fuller, J., and Farrington, J. *From Training to Performance Improvement: Navigating the Transition.* San Francisco: Pfeiffer, 1999.

LaGrossa, V., and Saxe, S. *The Consultative Approach: Partnering for Results.* San Francisco: Pfeiffer, 1998.

Maister, David. H, Green, Charles H., and Galford, Robert M. *The Trusted Advisor.* New York: Free Press, 2000.

Pepitone, J. S. *Human Performance Consulting: Transforming Human Potential into Productive Business Performance.* Houston: Gulf Professional Publishing, 2000.

Robinson, D. G., and Robinson, J. C. (eds.) *Moving from Training to Performance: A Practical Guidebook.* San Francisco, CA: Berrett-Koehler Publishers, 1998.

Robinson, D. G., and Robinson, J. C. *Performance Consulting: Moving Beyond Training.* San Francisco: Berrett-Koehler Publishers, 1995.

Rosania, R. J. *The Credible Trainer: Create Value for Training, Get Approval for Your Ideas, and Boost Your Career.* Alexandria, VA: ASTD, 2000.

Rummler, G. A. *Serious Performance Consulting According to Rummler.* Silver Spring, MD: ISPI, 2004.

Schaffer, R. H. *High-Impact Consulting: How Clients and Consultants Can Work Together to Achieve Extraordinary Results* (rev. ed.). San Francisco, CA: Jossey-Bass, 2002.

Scott, B. *Consulting on the Inside: An Internal Consultant's Guide to Living and Working Inside Organizations.* Alexandria, VA: ASTD, 2000.

Thomas, M. *High-Performance Consulting Skills: The Internal Consultant's Guide to Value-Added Performance.* London, UK: Thorogood, 2004.

Weiss, A. *Organizational Consulting: How to Be an Effective Internal Change Agent.* New York: John Wiley & Sons, 2003.

Business Knowledge

Afuah, A. *Business Models: A Strategic Management Approach.* New York: Irwin/McGraw-Hill, 2003.

Beitler, M. A. *Strategic Organizational Change: A Practitioner's Guide for Managers and Consultants.* Greensboro, NC: Practitioner Press International, 2003.

Bossidy, L., and Charan, R. *Execution: The Discipline of Getting Things Done.* New York: Crown Business, 2002.

Browne, M. N., and Keeley, S. M. *Asking the Right Questions: A Guide to Critical Thinking.* New York: Prentice Hall, 2003.

Charan, R. *What the CEO Wants You to Know: Using Your Business Acumen to Understand How Your Company Really Works.* New York: Crown Business, 2001.

Collins, J. *Good to Great: Why Some Companies Make the Leap...and Others Don't.* New York, NY: HarperCollins Publishers, 2001.

Freedman, M. *The Art and Discipline of Strategic Leadership.* New York: McGraw-Hill Companies, 2002.

Kaplan, R. S., and Norton, D. P. *The Strategy-Focused Organization: How Balanced Scorecard Companies Thrive in the New Business Environment.* Boston: Harvard Business School Press, 2000.

Kaufman, R., Oakley-Brown, Watkins, R., and Leigh, D. *Strategic Planning for Success: Aligning People, Performance and Payoffs.* San Francisco: Pfeiffer, 2003.

Kouzes, J. M., and Posner, B. Z. *Credibility: How Leaders Gain and Lose It, Why People Demand It.* New York: John Wiley & Sons, 2003.

Mitchell, D., and Coles, C. *The Ultimate Competitive Advantage: Secrets of Continually Developing a More Profitable Business Model.* San Francisco: Berrett-Koehler Publishers, 2003.

Reardon, K. K. *The Secret Handshake: Mastering the Politics of the Business Inner Circle.* New York: Doubleday Publishing, 2002.

Rothschild, W. E. *Putting It All Together: A Guide to Strategic Thinking and Decision Making.* Norwalk, CT: Rothschild Strategies Unlimited LLC, 2002.

Seagraves, T. *Quick! Show Me Your Value.* Alexandria, VA: ASTD Press, 2004.

Ulrich, D., and Smallwood, N. *Why the Bottom Line ISN'T!: How to Build Value Through People and Organization.* New York: John Wiley & Sons, 2003.

ASSOCIATIONS

Academy of Human Resource Development (AHRD)

The Academy of Human Resource Development was formed to encourage systematic study of human resource theories, processes, and practices; to disseminate information about HRD, to encourage the application of HRD research findings, and to provide opportunities for social interaction among individuals with scholarly and professional interests in HRD from multiple disciplines and from across the globe.

website: www.ahrd.org

ASTD

ASTD is a leading association of workplace learning and performance professionals, forming a world-class community of practice from more than 100 countries and thousands of organizations. ASTD's mission is to create a world that works better through exceptional learning and performance.

website: www.astd.org

Human Resource Planning Society (HRPS)

HRPS is a non-profit organization representing a mix of leading-edge thinkers and practitioners in business, industry, consulting and academia around the world. HRPS is committed to improving organizational performance by creating a global network of individuals who function as business partners in the application of strategic human resource management practices to their organizations.

website: www.hrps.org

International Society for Performance Improvement (ISPI)

ISPI is the leading international association dedicated to improving productivity and performance in the workplace. ISPI's mission is to develop and recognize the proficiency of its members and advocate the use of Human Performance Technology-a systematic approach to improving productivity and competence.

website: www.ispi.org

Organization Development Network (OD Network)

The OD Network is a vital learning community that develops, supports, and inspires practitioners and enhances the body of knowledge in human organization and systems development. It leads the Organization Development field and its practitioners in creating effective and healthy human systems in an inclusive world community.

website: www.ODNetwork.org

Society for Human Resource Management (SHRM)

SHRM serves the needs of the human resource management professional by providing the most essential and comprehensive set of resources available. In addition, the Society is committed to advancing the human resource profession and the capabilities of all human resource professionals to ensure that HR is an essential and effective partner in developing and executing organizational strategy.

website: www.shrm.org

Index

"Burning platform," 151

Business goals, methods for determining, 145–148, 149

Business knowledge, 73–74, 141
and credibility, 72–77, 82
methods for developing, 75–76
resources on, 268–269

Business needs, 15–16, 17, 21, 22

Business partner, defined, viii

Business plan(s)
accountability and measurement of results, 205–208
communication of to HR colleagues, 198
integration of HR strategic plan into, 46, 50, 197–200, 201–203, 208, 223–224
people initiatives in, 46–48, 50, 199–200, 203–205
role of SBP in formation of, 44, 50, 191–197

Business strategy
defined, 149
formation of, 196–197

C

Capability needs, 17, 19, 20, 22, 118

Cause analysis, 161, 170, 185

Cause questions, 24, 94–95, 96, 104, 192

Centers of Excellence (COEs), 222

Change management, 78

Client(s)
alternate terms for, 54
defined, 26
gaining access to, steps in, 56, 70

identification of, 10, 26–27, 29, 53
in implementation of strategic projects, 41, Lawler, 43
in proactive identification of strategic opportunities, 40
project, 26–27, 61–62
requests from, 89–90
satisfaction, 181
sustained, 26, 54–57
transitioning from tactical to strategic relationships, 57

Client partnerships
building, 35–37, 49–50
purpose of, 38
to support strategic projects, 38–41

Client requests, reframing, 39–40, 107–135

Coaching and reinforcement, 19, 167

Collaboration, 64

Communication
of business plan to HR colleagues, 198
importance of, 204, 230–231

Compaq, 191

Competency model, 160, 185

Competing model, 160, 185

Concept, defined, 10

Consulting, 76, 84
resources on, 267–268

Consulting model, 78

"Corporate attic," 2

Credibility, 35–36, 49, 52
business knowledge and, 72–77, 82

About the Authors

Dana Gaines Robinson and Jim Robinson are the President and Chairman, respectively, of Partners in Change, Inc., a consulting firm formed in 1981. Based in Pittsburgh, Pennsylvania, the firm provides services to organizations around the world. Among the many clients of the Robinsons are Allied-Domecq, The Gillette Company, Johnson Controls, Wachovia Corporation, and the YMCA. Both Dana and Jim are frequent speakers at national and international conferences.

Prior to teaming up in Partners in Change, Dana was an internal Human Resource professional for several years. She led the learning organizations in both a financial and pharmaceutical corporation. Jim was a Vice President at Development Dimensions International (DDI), where he was the primary architect for its most successful training program, Interaction Management.

Together the Robinsons have coauthored and coedited several books including *Training for Impact, Moving from*

Training to Performance and the award-winning book *Performance Consulting*. With Ken Blanchard they coauthored the book *Zap the Gaps! Target Higher Performance and Achieve It!* Collectively, their books have been translated into more than 20 languages. They have been awarded ASTD's Distinguished Contribution to Workplace Learning and Performance as well as the Thought Leadership Award from ISA.

When not writing or consulting, the Robinsons thoroughly enjoy their time with family, which includes seven grandchildren. They are also world travelers, having visited more than 40 countries to date and with plans to visit others.

Services Available

Partners in Change, Inc., is a recognized leader in the area of performance technology, working with clients to ensure that employee performance is linked to and directly supportive of business goals. The process the Robinsons have helped to develop, Performance Consulting, is currently utilized by thousands of HR, Learning, and OD professionals worldwide. The services provided by Partners in Change include:

- Assistance to HR, Learning, and OD functions as they design and implement a transition to a more strategic, business-linked approach.

- Consultation services to assist teams to identify and address performance gaps that are having a detrimental impact upon achievement of business goals.

- Skill-building workshops to build the capability of HR, Learning, and OD professionals in how to consult with managers on strategic initiatives.

For more information about the services that Jim and Dana Robinson provide, please visit their Web site at www.partners-in-change.com or contact them directly at:

> Partners in Change, Inc.
> 105 Trenton Circle
> McMurray, PA 15317-3657
> Phone: 412-854-5750
> Fax: 724-942-7768
> E-mail: mail@partners-in-change.com

Evaluating Training Programs
The Four Levels, 2nd Edition

Donald L. Kirkpatrick

A comprehensive step-by-step guide to evaluating training programs-from the creator of the "Kirkpatrick Model," the most widely used approach for evaluating training programs in industry, business, government, and academic institutions.

Hardcover, 308 pages • ISBN 1-57675-042-6 • Item #50426 $39.95

Transferring Learning to Behavior
Using the Four Levels to Improve Performance

Donald L. Kirkpatrick and James D. Kirkpatrick

Training professionals are under tremendous pressure to demonstrate the value of training to organizational executives. This book operationalizes Donald Kirkpatrick's Four Level model of training evaluation to meet that directive by comprehensively first attacking the great challenge of getting managers and employees to apply (Level 3) what they have learned (Level 2).

Hardcover, 240 pages • ISBN 978-1-57675-325-5 • Item #93225 $39.95

The Professional Trainer
A Comprehensive Guide to Planning, Delivering, and Evaluating Training Programs

Robert H. Vaughn

Written for the first-time trainer, this is a concise, "hands-on" overview of the training field. Drawing upon years of experience as a trainer in both the private and public sectors, Vaughn provides many specific examples and applications within the text and in helpful appendices in this revised and updated classic.

Paperback, 264 pages • ISBN 978-1-57675-270-8 • Item #92708 $29.95

Berrett-Koehler Publishers
PO Box 565, Williston, VT 05495-9900
Call toll-free! **800-929-2929** 7 am-9 pm EST
Or fax your order to 1-802-864-7626
For fastest service order online: **www.bkconnection.com**

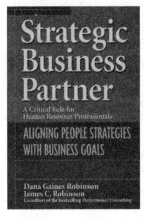